HOW TO FIND COURAGE WHEN ALL YOU HAVE IS YOU:

A TIMELESS GUIDE TO BUILD RESILIENCE, OVERCOME SELF-DOUBT, AND IGNITE YOUR INNER STRENGTH, SO YOU CAN FOCUS ON WHAT TRULY MATTERS

ARLENE GRACE EVANGELISTA

© **Copyright Arlene Grace Evangelista 2025 - All rights reserved.**

The content within this book may not be reproduced, duplicated or transmitted without direct written permission from the author or the publisher.

Under no circumstances will any blame or legal responsibility be held against the publisher, or author, for any damages, reparation, or monetary loss due to the information contained within this book. Either directly or indirectly. You are responsible for your own choices, actions, and results.

Legal Notice:

This book is copyright-protected. This book is only for personal use. You cannot amend, distribute, sell, use, quote, or paraphrase any part, of the content within this book, without the consent of the author or publisher.

Disclaimer Notice:

Please note the information contained within this document is for educational and entertainment purposes only. All effort has been expended to present accurate, up-to-date, and reliable, complete information. No warranties of any kind are declared or implied. Readers acknowledge that the author is not engaging in the rendering of legal, financial, medical or professional advice. The content within this book has been derived from various sources. Please consult a licensed professional before attempting any techniques outlined in this book.

By reading this document, the reader agrees that under no circumstances is the author responsible for any losses, direct or indirect, which are incurred as a result of the use of the information contained within this document, including, but not limited to, — errors, omissions, or inaccuracies.

I sincerely thank you for choosing to read this book. Your willingness to explore the path of emotional courage is a testament to your strength and growth. I hope these pages inspire, challenge, and empower you to face life with resilience and authenticity. May you find the wisdom, clarity, and courage you seek, and may this book guide your journey. Thank you for your trust in allowing my words to be a part of your story.

To my family, Limer, Maurice, Nic, and Bella, you are always my inspiration. With you, I can make my dreams possible.

CONTENTS

Introduction   7

1. EMBRACING EMOTIONAL INTELLIGENCE   11
   1.1 Understanding Your Emotional Landscape   12
   1.2 Strategies for Emotional Awareness   13
   1.3 Balancing Emotion and Logic   15
   1.4 Enhancing Empathy for Stronger Connections   17
   1.5 Emotional Regulation Techniques   19
   1.6 Building Emotional Resilience Through Mindfulness   20

2. DEVELOPING A GROWTH MINDSET   25
   2.1 The Science of a Growth Mindset   26
   2.2 Techniques for Shifting Perspectives   28
   2.3 Overcoming Fear of Failure   30
   2.4 Embracing Challenges as Opportunities   32
   2.5 Building Resilience Through Learning   33
   2.6 Celebrating Small Wins   35

3. PRACTICAL STRATEGIES FOR OVERCOMING SELF-DOUBT   39
   3.1 Identifying and Challenging Self-Talk   40
   3.2 Cognitive-Behavioral Techniques for Confidence   42
   3.3 Visualization for Succes   44
   3.4 Setting and Achieving Personal Goals   45
   3.5 Mastering Positive Self-Reinforcement   47
   3.6 Building Confidence Through Competence   48

4. NAVIGATING LIFE TRANSITIONS WITH COURAGE   53
   4.1 Embracing Change and Uncertainty   54
   4.2 Frameworks for Decision-Making in Transitions   56
   4.3 Creating Adaptable Plans for Change   58
   4.4 Managing Stress in Transitional Phases   59
   4.5 Finding Opportunity in New Beginnings   63

5. BUILDING A SUPPORTIVE COMMUNITY   69
   5.1 The Power of Connection   70
   5.2 Building and Nurturing Relationships   72
   5.3 Creating a Tribe of Support   74

5.4 Networking with Intention and Purpose	75
5.5 Mutual Growth Through Community Building	77
5.6 Leveraging Support Networks for Resilience	79
6. INTEGRATING MINDFULNESS AND SELF-CARE	**83**
6.1 The Role of Mindfulness in Resilience	84
6.2 Self-Care Practices for Emotional Health	86
6.3 Mindfulness Meditation Techniques	88
6.4 Journaling for Self-Reflection and Growth	90
6.5 Balancing Mind and Body Wellness	91
6.6 Sustaining Well-being Through Daily Rituals	93
7. HARNESSING REAL-LIFE NARRATIVES	**97**
7.1 Learning from Inspirational Leaders	98
7.2 Overcoming Adversity: Personal Success Stories	100
7.4 Transformative Journeys from Helplessness to Hope	104
7.5 Lessons in Resilience from Diverse Perspectives	106
7.6 Applying Insights from Inspirational Stories	108
8. ACHIEVING LONG-TERM TRANSFORMATION	**113**
8.1 Sustaining Change Through Consistency	114
8.2 Long-Term Strategies for Emotional Growth	116
8.3 Cultivating a Life of Purpose and Meaning	118
8.4 Embracing Vulnerability as Strength	120
8.5 The Journey to Authentic Empowerment	121
Conclusion	125
A Journey's End, A New Beginning	129
References	131

INTRODUCTION

"While working my shift at the fast-food front counter, surrounded by the fryer's hum and the register's occasional beep, a moment arrived that would reshape my life forever. My supervisor approached me with a look that I'd never seen before, delivering the incomprehensible news: my father had passed away. Just three weeks after his 40th birthday, with no warning or illness, how could he suddenly *be gone? The drive home felt endless, the weight of confusion pressing down on me as my mind spiraled with fear and unanswered questions. What had happened to him? What will happen to us? He was the sole provider for our family. Questions about our future, our schooling, and how we could possibly keep it all together raced through my mind, each one more impossible than the last. Arriving home to the sight of my family in tears—my mother, my siblings, my three younger brothers, and my sister—**I felt a profound sense of helplessness, and an overwhelming need to be responsible. Holding my youngest siblings, ages three and six, I wondered if they understood the tragedy that had happened to us. Were they experiencing the same depth of pain as I was feeling?** At that moment, though I was still so young, something was clear: I had to grow up fast and step into a role that seemed too big for me. I had to embody strength, not just for myself, but as the new head of my family. In the face of our collective grief, I found no time to cry because my mind was occupied. **I don't remember shedding tears. The gentle and warm touch of my younger brothers' hands didn't just comfort me; it sparked a determination I hadn't known I possessed. I had to muster courage, not just for my sake, but for theirs.** That pivotal day in April marked the beginning of my journey toward courage and resilience."*

This guide is crafted for those moments when isolation and self-doubt cloud your spirit, leaving you feeling lost and uncertain. If feelings of isolation or questions of self-worth have ever clouded your vision, this book offers hope. Within its pages lies a transformative journey designed to fortify your resilience, conquer self-doubt, and awaken the potent force of inner strength that resides quietly within you.

This book is a guide for both men and women who are battling with the weight of isolation in their struggles. Whether it's personal loss, separation, abandonment, business failure, or the exhaustion of a once-passionate career, these burdens can seem impossible to overcome. The essence of this guide is to navigate you towards harnessing emotional courage. It transforms the narrative from weakening and despair to finding an internal source of strength and hope. Remember, you are not navigating this journey alone. There are so many of us. This work aims to be a source of empowerment, encouraging you to rise, reclaim the strength that you once had, and embark on a path of positive transformation.

Throughout this book, I share personal anecdotes from my journey. These experiences aren't meant to overshadow your own but to offer relatable examples that can guide you on your path to discovering your courageous self. The guide is thoughtfully structured around pivotal themes and topics, including the cultivation of emotional intelligence, the fostering of a growth mindset, and the importance of forging meaningful connections. Every chapter is rich with insights and actionable strategies, designed not only to enlighten but also to make your journey toward resilience as compelling as it is enlightening.

What sets this writing apart is its foundation in research-backed strategies, ensuring that the tools and techniques you learn here are both practical and effective. The content ensures that the guidance you receive is inspiring and proven. To make these strategies easier to apply in your daily life, I've included real-world scenarios that show how they can be used to overcome your challenges.

Let me share a bit about myself. My career as an immigration professional has been driven by a fervent passion for guiding others through transformative life journeys. Years of dedication to this work have been fueled by a profound commitment to making a significant, positive difference in the lives of my clients. This commitment stems from a heartfelt wish to see every person I assist flourish and enhance their quality of life. The research behind this book is rooted in my desire to offer a helping hand, guiding you with direction and support during your current struggles.

As you turn the pages, you'll uncover actionable strategies for building resilience and pathways that inspire self-discovery, guiding you toward a life of greater harmony. The insights shared here transcend mere advice; these are practical tools for profound transformation. I believe that we can all achieve a kind of life not just to get by—but one that is defined by personal comfort and well-being, in whatever form that may take. If this book helps even one reader, bringing them emotional or mental peace, then it serves the value of my effort. This belief fuels my commitment to making a meaningful impact through my words.

I invite you to engage actively with the content of this material. Reflect on the stories and techniques presented here. Integrate them into your daily life, test their strength, and watch how they help you turn obstacles into opportunities for growth. This manuscript is more than a mere reference; it's a perpetual companion for those moments when your resolve wavers and despair sets in.

The journey of personal transformation is filled with moments of doubt and courage. This guide will show you the way, helping you tap into the strength you already possess to face these challenges with courage. Together, we step into this journey, seeking the courage that we know we have. **Let us start to live not just to get by in life but to reach our highest potential.** The first step? Belief in our power to effect change, we must sincerely believe that we will make things happen for us and find the courageous self we are hiding.

Let's do it together.

1

EMBRACING EMOTIONAL INTELLIGENCE

"Years ago, I experienced a particularly devastating day when I received harrowing news: my father had been attacked by robbers. The assailant made off with a clutch bag filled with cash and jewelry, as reported by the police. At that moment, the weight of reality was suffocating. The truth was tangible, and my instinct was to blame someone, but I didn't know whom to blame. All I remember was trying to breathe, but I couldn't. I felt a profound sense of helplessness."

My emotional turmoil wasn't about assigning fault—it was about confronting my deep-seated feelings of inadequacy. This realization revealed that I was unprepared for the enormity of my situation. This insight was a small yet significant step into understanding emotional intelligence—a realm where emotions are felt, understood, and managed with intention. **This moment led me to a deeper understanding of emotional intelligence (EI)—the ability to recognize, understand, and manage both our own emotions and those of others.**

1.1 UNDERSTANDING YOUR EMOTIONAL LANDSCAPE

As defined by Daniel Goleman, emotional intelligence includes five key components: **self-awareness, self-regulation, motivation, empathy, and social skills. Self-awareness** is the ability to recognize your emotions as they occur. It is the foundation of EI, allowing you to understand your strengths, weaknesses, and triggers. **Self-regulation** involves managing emotions and impulses and maintaining control even in challenging situations. **Motivation** refers to the intrinsic drive to achieve goals, while **empathy** is the capacity to understand and share the feelings of others. **Social skills** encompass the ability to build relationships and navigate social environments effectively. These components work together, creating a framework for effective emotional navigation.

Self-reflection is a crucial tool for developing emotional intelligence. This process involves examining your thoughts, emotions, and behaviors to gain insight into your emotional responses. **Journaling** is a powerful method of self-reflection, allowing you to process emotions and identify reaction patterns. When you write about your emotional triggers, you see the connections between events and your emotional responses. This practice can help clarify why certain situations provoke strong emotions, providing a roadmap for managing these feelings in the future.

Recognizing emotional triggers is essential to understanding your emotions. These triggers can be specific situations, interactions, or thoughts that elicit strong emotional responses. In the workplace, common triggers include receiving critical feedback, dealing with high-pressure deadlines, or navigating office politics. In personal relationships, stressors can arise from misunderstandings, unmet expectations, conflicts with family members, or even the fear of abandonment. By identifying these triggers, you can develop strategies to manage them, gaining a greater sense of control over your emotions.

Our past experiences greatly influence our emotional responses and perceptions. Childhood influences, for example, often leave lasting impressions on how we process emotions. If you grew up in an environment where your family members did not openly express their emotions, you might find it challenging to articulate your feelings as an adult. Alternatively, positive early experiences with emotional expression can foster a healthy understanding of emotions. **Reflecting on these experiences can make you more self-aware and reflective, helping you understand how they influence your emotional landscape.**

Reflecting on Emotional Triggers

Take a moment to think about a recent situation that triggered a strong emotional response. Write down the event's details, your initial reaction, and any underlying thoughts or feelings that might have contributed to this response. Consider whether this situation mirrors past experiences or highlights an area where you can grow emotionally. Use this exercise to deepen your understanding of how past experiences shape your present emotional landscape. **Reflecting on these triggers** helps you better understand your emotions and their impact on your behavior. This is the first step toward managing them with greater awareness and control.

As we navigate this chapter, you will learn how to cultivate each aspect of emotional intelligence, empowering you to face life's challenges with resilience. Understanding and managing your emotional landscape sets the stage for personal growth and gives you a profound sense of control and confidence in your interactions with others.

1.2 STRATEGIES FOR EMOTIONAL AWARENESS

> *"Imagine sitting at the bench of your confusion and uncertainties. People bombard you with advice: 'Get a lawyer.' 'This was targeted.' 'Demand payment.' 'Settle.' 'Go here, do this, do that.' Their voices blur into static, and you struggle to process their words"*

Finding a moment to pause and observe without judgment in this chaos can seem impossible, yet this practice is precisely at the heart of emotional awareness.

Mindful observation involves noticing your emotions as they arise, much like watching traffic from the sidewalk—observing without being swept into the flow. You allow yourself to experience feelings without labeling them as good or bad. This practice fosters a present-moment awareness that encourages a deeper understanding of your emotional states.

Labeling emotions accurately is another crucial step in developing emotional literacy, a key component of emotional intelligence. Emotional literacy involves recognizing your feelings and naming them. It's about understanding nuances—such as distinguishing between anger and frustration—and recognizing how they manifest in your body and mind. This understanding can significantly affect how you address them. **Anger** might signal a boundary violation, while **frustration** often arises from unmet expectations. Labeling these emotions gives you the clarity needed to respond effectively. This practice enhances your emotional vocabulary, enabling you to articulate your feelings more accurately in conversations. **A broad emotional vocabulary acts as a lens, intensifying your internal world.**

Incorporating daily emotional check-ins can further deepen your emotional awareness. Consider starting and ending each day with a simple self-assessment. Upon waking, ask yourself how you feel and what emotions are present. In the evening, reflect on the day's events and your emotional responses to them. Ask yourself what triggered these emotions and how you could have responded differently. These check-ins keep you attuned to your emotional reality and reveal patterns in your habitual reactions. Over time, you may notice patterns in your emotional responses, which can guide you in developing more applicable coping strategies.

Expanding your emotional vocabulary is like giving a painter more colors to work with. Each new word offers a distinct hue, enriching the canvas of your emotional expression. You better understand yourself as you learn to use nuanced language to describe your emotions. Instead of saying you're 'upset,' you might identify feelings of disappointment, irritation, or disillusionment—each requiring a different response. Such specificity fosters a tighter connection to your emotional experiences and enhances your ability to communicate them to others.

Emotional Vocabulary Expansion Exercise

Take a moment to write down your emotions from the past week. Use a thesaurus or emotion chart to find more precise words to describe each one. Reflect on how these words change your understanding of your experiences. Consider how you might use this expanded vocabulary in future interactions. This exercise builds emotional awareness and improves your ability to connect with others through more transparent communication.

As you cultivate these strategies, you begin to see emotions as valuable data guiding your decisions and interactions. By practicing observation, labeling, checking in, and expanding your emotional vocabulary, you develop a deeper emotional awareness that enhances every aspect of your life.

1.3 BALANCING EMOTION AND LOGIC

Emotions and logic often pull us in opposite directions in the complex decision-making process. Yet, they can work harmoniously with each other when balanced. Imagine standing at a crossroads, where each path offers risk and reward. Your heart urges you toward a choice driven by passion while your mind calculates the potential outcomes precisely. This scenario is where a decision-making framework, one that respects both emotion and logic, becomes invaluable. One practical tool is a pros and cons list—but with an added layer: **emotional weighting**. This method itemizes each option's benefits and drawbacks and considers each factor's emotional significance. By assigning a weight to how each pro or con makes you feel, you gain a clearer picture of what is truly important to you. This approach helps illuminate a path that aligns with your rational goals and emotional desires.

Consider the story of a business person faced with a high-stress decision about whether to expand her company into an unpredictable market. The numbers suggested potential growth on paper, yet her intuition whispered caution, recalling a past venture that ended in turmoil. By employing a balanced decision-making framework, she listed the tangible pros: market demand, potential revenue, and strategic positioning. She noted the cons: financial risk, operational strains, and the emotional toll of previous failures. Each factor was then emotionally weighted, acknowledging her fear of repeating past mistakes and her excitement about new possibilities. This process allowed her to gauge her analytical insights and emotional instincts, ultimately leading to a calculated decision considering every angle.

In personal life, the same balanced approach can transform uncertainty into clarity. Picture someone considering a move to a new city torn between the potential opportunity and the comfort of familiarity. Here, the pros and cons list with emotional weighting reveals deeper insights. The list might include pros like career advancement, cultural experiences, and personal growth, while the cons feature homesickness, financial uncertainty, and loss of community. They see each choice's logical implications and emotional resonance by evaluating each point through an emotional lens. This understanding guides them in making decisions that respect their aspirations and their need for emotional stability.

Practical Exercise: Balancing Emotion and Logic

To integrate this balance into your daily life, try this exercise next time you face a difficult decision. Start by crafting a **simple pros and cons list** for each option. Once completed, take a moment to reflect on how each point makes you feel. **Assign an emotional weight** from one to five, where one is low emotional impact, and five is high. This weighting system allows you to see beyond the surface and understand which aspects hold the most emotional significance. Consider how these emotions align with your values and goals. This exercise not only clarifies your decision-making process but also strengthens your ability to tackle complexities with confidence.

Balancing emotion and logic is not about eliminating one in favor of the other. It is about weaving them together, creating a decision that reflects your head and heart. **When you allow emotion to inform logic and vice versa, your decisions become more holistic and authentic.** This approach directs you to make well-reasoned choices that align with your identity. In this balance, emotion and logic find their rightful place, guiding you toward decisions that resonate on every level.

1.4 ENHANCING EMPATHY FOR STRONGER CONNECTIONS

Empathy goes beyond understanding another person's feelings—it is the foundation of meaningful relationships. Empathy serves as a bridge in a world where misunderstandings often lead to conflict. It allows us to step into another's experience, offering a perspective that removes our biases. Empathy can turn disagreements into constructive dialogues, facilitating solutions and easing conflicts by ensuring everyone feels acknowledged. Practicing empathy fosters genuine connections and promotes understanding.

Active listening is a powerful technique to enhance empathy. It requires more than simply hearing words; it involves engaging with the speaker's message and responding thoughtfully. One effective method is paraphrasing and summarizing the speaker's words, confirming understanding and demonstrating engagement. For instance, during a heated discussion with a loved one, you might say, "So, what I'm hearing is It is not you don't want to undergo treatment, but you're concerned about the cost, and you are scared to be blamed if the treatment doesn't work." This approach validates the other person's feelings, paving the way for more constructive interactions. **By actively listening, you convey respect and build trust, two essential components of any strong relationship.**

To deepen your empathetic abilities, consider engaging in **perspective-taking exercises**. These activities challenge you to view the world through someone else's eyes. One such exercise is the "**walking in someone else's shoes**" activity. Choose a person whose experiences differ from yours and imagine their daily life. Consider the challenges they face, the motivations behind their actions, and the context of their decisions. By challenging your biases, this practice broadens your understanding of others' experiences, fostering deeper connections.

Regularly considering different perspectives helps develop a mindset that values diversity and empathy. This is especially important in team settings, where successful collaboration often relies on members' understanding and relating to each other. Take, for example, a group tasked with completing a complex project under a tight deadline. Each team member brings unique skills and perspectives, and empathy becomes the glue that holds the project together. When conflicts arise, empathetic team members listen actively, acknowledge differing viewpoints, and work collectively toward a solution that respects everyone's contributions. This collaboration enhances the team's effectiveness and strengthens the bonds between its members.

Empathy Exercise: Active Listening Practice

To practice active listening, choose a conversation partner and focus entirely on their words. As they speak, refrain from interrupting or formulating your response. Instead, please pay attention to their tone, body language, and emotions. Once they finish, paraphrase their message to confirm your understanding. This exercise strengthens your listening skills and fosters a deeper connection with the speaker. You create an atmosphere where meaningful connections can flourish by prioritizing empathy in your interactions.

As you integrate these practices into your daily life, you will notice an improvement in how you relate to others. **Empathy becomes a lens through which you view the world, offering clarity and depth to your relationships.** Whether in personal or professional settings, the ability to empathize enriches your interactions, allowing you to connect with others on a meaningful level. In cultivating empathy, you enhance your relationships and contribute to a more understanding and compassionate world.

1.5 EMOTIONAL REGULATION TECHNIQUES

"Imagine standing at your father's funeral, grief tightening around your chest. Then, you notice someone who shouldn't be there—a presence that ignites something raw inside you, an anger simmering just beneath the surface."

Emotional regulation manages these feelings, allowing us to maintain balance despite external chaos. It involves controlling emotional impulses to prevent regretful decisions, like adjusting a volume dial to maintain balance when emotions surge. Emotional regulation is essential for healthy interactions, sound decisions, and overall well-being. By learning to regulate emotions, we create a more harmonious internal environment, influencing how we engage with the world.

One of the most accessible techniques for regulating emotions is through **breathing and relaxation**. Deep breathing exercises are a simple yet effective way to calm the mind and body. Start by sitting comfortably, closing your eyes, and taking a slow, deep breath through your nose. Hold it for a moment, then exhale gently through your mouth. Repeat this process several times, allowing each breath to do its wonders. This technique helps lower heart rate and reduce stress, making it easier to manage emotional responses. **Progressive muscle relaxation** offers another calming strategy. In this practice, you systematically tense and then relax different muscle groups, starting from your toes and moving upward. This approach relieves physical tension and promotes mental relaxation, helping you stay grounded during intense emotional moments.

Cognitive reframing is another powerful tool in emotional regulation. It involves shifting your perspective on a situation to alter its emotional impact. Consider a challenge that initially seems unachievable. Reframing it as a learning opportunity transforms anxiety into curiosity and fear into motivation. This approach helps you view setbacks as chances to grow rather than failures. When faced with challenges, take a moment to ask yourself: What can I learn from this? How can this experience help me grow? **By reframing challenges, you empower yourself to navigate them with resilience and optimism.**

Relaxation Techniques

Stress reduction is integral to emotional regulation. Everyday life presents an array of stressors, from looming deadlines to personal commitments. Adding practical stress-management techniques to your routine can help you handle these demands more smoothly. **Physical activity** like walking or yoga releases endorphins that improve mood and reduce stress hormones. **Scheduling regular breaks** during work can also lower stress levels, allowing you to recharge mentally and physically. Another method is engaging in **activities that bring joy and relaxation**, whether reading, gardening, or listening to music. These moments of relief act as pressure valves, releasing built-up tension and restoring balance.

Emotional regulation techniques do not involve suppressing feelings but guiding them in a way that serves your well-being. By integrating breathing exercises, cognitive reframing, and stress reduction practices into your life, you cultivate resilience that empowers you to face challenges with composure. These techniques become second nature with practice, providing stability during emotional ups and downs.

1.6 BUILDING EMOTIONAL RESILIENCE THROUGH MINDFULNESS

Mindfulness is like standing in the eye of a storm, where the winds of stress howl around you, yet you remain still, untouched by the chaos. It is best described as fully present in each moment, acknowledging it without judgment. This practice promotes calmness and clarity, making it a valuable tool for emotional resilience. Mindfulness builds awareness, helping us respond to stress thoughtfully rather than reacting impulsively. It fosters acceptance, supports a balanced approach to challenges, and strengthens our ability to recover from setbacks.

Integrating mindfulness into daily life begins with simple practices. **Mindfulness** sharpens awareness, allowing us to approach stress with intention rather than knee-jerk reactions. One such practice is the **body scan meditation**, where you mentally scan your body from head to toe, noting areas of tension or discomfort. Focusing on each part creates a sense of presence and relaxation. **Loving-kindness meditation** is another helpful practice that silently repeats phrases of goodwill toward yourself and others. It promotes compassion and empathy, enhances emotional resilience, and strengthens relationships.

Mindfulness is not confined to meditation alone. It can be integrated into daily activities, turning routine tasks into moments of awareness. Take **mindful eating**, for instance. Slowly enjoy each bite instead of rushing through meals, noticing the flavors, textures, and aromas. This practice improves your dining experience and promotes healthier eating habits. Similarly, mindful walking means tuning into each step, the rhythm of your breath, and the surrounding world. By walking mindfully, you connect with your environment and yourself, finding peace in motion.

The real power of mindfulness becomes evident when applied to real-life challenges. Right now, I'm navigating a stressful workload—preparing year-end paperwork for my accountant, renewing licenses and insurance, studying a proof of concept for my research, and reviewing multiple applications for submission. I incorporated mindfulness into my routine, beginning each day with a brief meditation. This small change helped me tackle tasks with a clear mind and less anxiety. By practicing mindful breathing during stressful moments, I noticed a difference in how I responded. Instead of feeling overwhelmed, I became more focused and resilient, managing pressure more effectively. This experience shows how mindfulness can change how we handle stress, building resilience through simple activities that easily fit into our daily routines.

Practicing mindful breathing in stressful moments transformed how I responded, making me more present and composed. This awareness helps us face challenges with resilience and transform obstacles into opportunities for growth.

As we continue cultivating mindfulness in our lives, we build a foundation of strength and stability, enabling us to face whatever comes our way. In this practice, we find a tool for managing stress and a path to greater emotional well-being and fulfillment.

Emotional intelligence serves as the foundation for personal growth and inner strength.

The Power Within:

Through storms of fear and silent doubt
I stood alone, but not without.
Emotions surged, a tide so deep,
Yet strength arose from wounds that weep.
To know oneself, to feel, to see,
Is where the path to strength must be.

Awareness blooms in self-reflect,
A mirror held, a life dissect.
To name the fear, to face its light,
Is how we turn the dark to sight.
With every word, with every thought,
We shape the lessons struggle brought.

Through mindful breath and steady gaze,
We find the calm in fleeting days.
Observe the mind, release the weight,
Let moments shape what we create.
In every pause, in each deep sigh,
Resilience grows, it learns to fly.

Balance guides where reason sways,
A dance of heart and mind that stays.
We weigh the risk, we trust the spark,
A guiding flame within the dark.
In thoughtful steps, in choices made,
Both logic and emotion trade.

With empathy, we bridge the space,
A gentle touch, a slower pace.
To hear, to hold, to truly see,
Is where connection longs to be.
Each word exchanged, each bond that's grown,
Builds walls of trust from seeds once sown.

Through practice, growth begins to rise,
Like morning sun in hopeful skies.
Mindfulness, a steady hand,
A guiding force through shifting sand.
In self-care's arms, we find our way,
To strength that holds and fears allay.

2

DEVELOPING A GROWTH MINDSET

"Years ago, as a young student, I desperately needed a job to support my family of five. Lacking any discernible skills or talents that might secure even a minimum-wage position, all I had to rely on was my fierce determination to provide for my younger siblings and my mother, who was debilitated by the shock and grief of my father's passing. The necessity to transition from adolescence to adulthood was clear. I conditioned my mind that I could do it, be trained, be capable of learning, and meet the demands of a job suitable for someone my age. This conviction was all I had to fuel myself, nothing else. I was 18 years old."

2.1 THE SCIENCE OF A GROWTH MINDSET

My persistence was not an inborn skill but a belief in my capacity to improve—a core principle of the **growth mindset**. This mindset, unlike a fixed one, **embraces challenges as opportunities for development rather than threats to self-worth.** I realized that continuous learning brings me closer to mastering any skill. It highlights the importance of having a growth-focused mindset.

Recognizing the difference between a fixed and growth mindset is the first step in reshaping your approach to challenges and success. A **fixed mindset** is characterized by the belief that abilities and intelligence are static traits set in stone at birth. People with this mindset often avoid challenges, fearing failure reflects their self-worth. They may see effort as useless if they don't have natural talent.

In contrast, a growth mindset is a belief that skills and abilities can be developed through dedication and hard work. This perspective fosters a love for learning and resilience, seeing failures not as endpoints but as stepping stones. It encourages taking risks, knowing that effort leads to growth and that intelligence and talent are just the starting points.

Scientific studies illuminate the neuroscience behind learning and growth. At the heart of this is neuroplasticity, the brain's remarkable ability to reorganize itself by forming new neural connections in response to knowledge and experience. This means that our brains are not fixed but adaptable throughout our lives. The more we engage in deliberate practice and learning, the more we strengthen these neural pathways, enhancing our cognitive capabilities. Research shows enriched environments can increase synaptic connections, demonstrating the brain's capacity to evolve with experience. **This adaptability is a powerful argument for the growth mindset, proving that change and improvement are always possible with the right mindset and effort.**

The impact of mindset on success is profound. Carol Dweck's research reveals that individuals with a growth mindset tend to achieve more than those with a fixed mindset because they focus on learning rather than merely looking smart. They understand that effort leads to mastery, viewing challenges as opportunities to expand their abilities. This mindset fosters resilience, as setbacks are valuable learning experiences rather than insurmountable failures. Students with a growth mindset show greater motivation and improved performance in educational settings. In professional environments, employees who embrace this mindset are more likely to take on challenges, innovate, and thrive.

Having a growth mindset is key to overcoming challenges. It builds resilience, helping individuals push through difficult times. History offers countless examples of individuals who embodied a growth mindset, turning obstacles into stepping stones. **Nelson Mandela,** for example, exhibited an unwavering growth mindset during his 27 years of imprisonment, using the time to reflect, learn, and prepare for leadership. His perseverance ultimately led to profound personal growth and societal change. Similarly, **Malala Yousafzai's** journey demonstrates how a growth mindset fuels resilience. She stayed dedicated to education and advocacy, turning her challenges into opportunities for global impact. These examples illustrate how a growth mindset empowers individuals to navigate adversity with courage and determination, seeing challenges as opportunities for transformation. Other notable figures with a growth mindset include **Thomas Edison,** who famously said, 'I have not failed. I've just found 10,000 ways that won't work,' and JK Rowling, who overcame rejection and poverty to become one of the most successful authors of our time. These individuals' stories are a testament to the power of a growth mindset in achieving success.

Reflection Section: Mindset Assessment

Take a moment to reflect on your current mindset. Consider a recent challenge and how you approached it. Did you see it as a chance to learn, or did you see it as something to avoid? Take a moment to write down your thoughts and consider where adopting a growth mindset could help you. Think about how this shift could change the way you handle future challenges. This exercise enables you to understand your current mindset and encourages positive changes toward growth and learning. To further assess and improve your mindset, try the following exercises: Three Good Things' exercise (writing down three positive things that happened during your day and why they happened), the 'Power of Yet' exercise (adding a word yet to a goal you haven't mastered, for example, "I can't speak publicly yet"), or the 'Mindful Breathing' exercise. These exercises will help you understand your current mindset and provide practical ways to shift toward a growth mindset.

Cultivating a growth mindset is not just a change in perspective; it's a profound transformation. It empowers you to embrace challenges, persist through setbacks, and continually evolve. By understanding the science and impact of this mindset, you unlock your potential to learn and grow, transforming obstacles into opportunities for advancement. This knowledge should inspire you, encourage you, and motivate you to start your journey of personal and professional growth.

2.2 TECHNIQUES FOR SHIFTING PERSPECTIVES

In our moments of self-reflection, many of us encounter a familiar challenge - **limiting beliefs**. These are the silent scripts that whisper, 'You're not good enough,' or 'You'll never succeed.' Recognizing these beliefs is the first step toward change—an eye-opening realization of the barriers holding you back. These beliefs often come from past experiences, societal expectations, or advice that, though well-meaning, left a lasting impact. For example, a bad experience can create a lifelong fear of public speaking. Recognizing these beliefs helps you understand how they have held you back and kept you from reaching your full potential.

Once you identify these limiting beliefs, the next step is to actively reshape them. This process is not just liberating; it's empowering. It allows you to take control of your personal growth and development. It enables you to actively shape your mindset and influence your future with confidence and intention.

Reframing negative thoughts is a powerful way to change your perspective and discover new possibilities. Start by catching yourself when you think, 'I can't,' and shift it to, 'I can learn how.' This simple shift in language can transform your mindset, fostering curiosity and openness to growth. For example, if you believe you're not good with numbers, change your mental language to "I can become better with practice and learning." This approach empowers you and fosters a personal drive to growth.

Gratitude is a powerful source of positivity, capable of reshaping even the most deeply rooted perspectives. When you practice gratitude, you shift your focus from what's missing to what's abundant in your life. Keeping a daily gratitude journal—even just a few sentences—can be a simple yet transformative habit. Each day, jot down three things you're thankful for—a supportive friend, a special time with your child, or indulging in your hobby. Over time, this practice trains your brain to seek the good, establishing a mindset of appreciation and positivity. It's a gentle reminder that, despite challenges, there is always something to be grateful for.

Visualization is a powerful technique that allows you to mentally rehearse success, making positive outcomes feel more achievable. Imagine yourself achieving a challenging goal, whether it's acing a presentation or completing a marathon. Picture the details—the sounds, the sights, the feelings of accomplishment. This exercise clarifies your vision and strengthens your motivation toward success. **Visualization isn't just daydreaming; it's a mental rehearsal that prepares you for real-world achievements.** Regularly engaging in this practice builds confidence and motivation, aligning your actions with your aspirations.

Visualization Exercise: Creating a Vision Board

Visualization is a powerful tool that shapes our reality. To tap into this power, create a vision board. Gather images, words, or symbols that represent your goals and dreams. Arrange them on a board where you can see them daily. This visual representation reminds you daily of your direction, keeping you focused and motivated to reach your goals. **As you achieve these goals, replace images with new ones, celebrating your progress and setting new missions.** This practice clarifies your intentions and fuels the action needed to turn your dreams into reality. Incorporating these techniques into your daily routine shifts **your perspective from limitation to possibility.** As you challenge limiting beliefs, reframe negative thoughts, practice gratitude, and visualize success, you cultivate a **mindset that embraces growth and transformation. These practices are tools and foundations for building a life of resilience, positivity, and achievement.**

2.3 OVERCOMING FEAR OF FAILURE

Imagine standing at the edge of a diving board; the pool below is inviting, but the jump is scary. The fear of leaping into the unknown mirrors the fear of failure we all encounter at some point in our lives. Yet, what if we redefined failure? Rather than seeing failure as a final end, reframe it as valuable feedback that directs you toward growth and improvement. **This shift in perspective transforms failure from a judgment of our abilities to a valuable learning experience.** When you begin to view failure as part of the journey, it becomes less intimidating and more of a necessary, empowering step in your growth. It invites curiosity, urging you to ask, "What can I learn from this?" rather than, "Why did I fail?"

Resilience is the remarkable inner strength that allows us to rise after every fall, to face setbacks not as defeats, but as opportunities to grow. It's not about avoiding failure but about **rising each time we stumble.** To cultivate resilience, immerse yourself in narratives of those who have thrived despite difficulties. Their stories ignite a spark within us, filling us with the energy and determination to press on. These resilience narratives emphasize that setbacks are not the end but a part of the journey toward success. When we see others overcome obstacles, it plants the seed of possibility within us, reminding us that we, too, can persevere.

When we analyze failure, we unlock valuable lessons that fuel our growth and understanding. The "What went wrong?" exercise is a simple yet effective framework for dissecting failures. Begin by identifying the outcome that fell short of your expectations. Next, explore the contributing factors—both external circumstances and your own actions or decisions that led to this outcome. Reflect on what could have been done differently and what lessons can be learned. This analysis not only helps you learn from past mistakes but also equips you with the strategies and mindset to achieve greater success moving forward. **You transform setbacks into stepping stones by framing failure as a learning opportunity.**

A strong support system is crucial—it not only helps you navigate failure but also provides the encouragement needed to rise again. Supportive individuals and experienced mentors can guide and motivate you during difficult times. Look for mentors who have faced obstacles and gained wisdom from their experiences. Their experiences offer valuable perspectives, guiding you through your journey. Mentors offer not only advice but also a sense of companionship, reminding you that you're never alone in your journey through struggle. Additionally, having a network of encouragers who believe in your ability can boost your confidence and encourage you. They act as your cheerleaders, celebrating every success and lifting you up during setbacks.

When you view failure through the **lens of opportunity** and surround yourself with **supportive individuals**, you create an environment conducive to growth. Embrace the lessons from each setback and allow them to shape your future challenges. **Failure becomes not a foe but a friend—a guide leading you toward a path of resilience and achievement.**

2.4 EMBRACING CHALLENGES AS OPPORTUNITIES

> " I came across an opportunity for a higher-paying position, but the selection process was daunting—a series of panel interviews. The thought of facing a formal job interview for the first time, let alone a panel, filled me with overwhelming fear and self-doubt. The very thought of it felt overwhelming; however, it is during moments of discomfort that true growth begins."

Facing challenges is not just about overcoming obstacles; it's about pushing the limits of what you once thought possible, expanding your potential in ways you never imagined. **Each time you venture beyond what is familiar, you stretch your capacity for resilience and adaptability**. This expansion leads to profound personal development, where the **limits you once accepted begin to dissolve**, opening up a world of new possibilities.

Setting stretch goals—goals that challenge you to go beyond your current abilities—is an effective way to cultivate growth and push your limits. These goals should be challenging yet attainable—designed to stretch your capabilities while still being within reach, ensuring they motivate rather than overwhelm you. The proven SMART goal framework can be instrumental here. It stands for Specific, Measurable, Achievable, Relevant, and Time-bound When you set goals that meet these criteria, you're not just creating a roadmap for success, but a clear path toward lasting growth and achievement. For instance, rather than setting a vague goal like "get fit," a SMART goal would be "run three miles twice a week for the next month." This clarity not only provides direction but also fuels motivation. As you work toward these goals, you build a track record of accomplishments that boost your confidence and encourage further growth.

Challenges often serve as triggers for innovation. When faced with a daunting problem, the mind is pushed to think outside the box, often finding creative solutions that were previously unimaginable. Take the story of a startup that reimagined its product to survive—a breakthrough made possible by adversity. Traditional methods had failed, and the team had no choice but to adapt. They reimagined their product, focusing on a niche market previously overlooked. This shift saved the company and opened new revenue streams, proving that adversity can be a fertile ground for innovation. **By embracing challenges, you tap into a source of creativity, finding better solutions that propel you forward.**

A shift in mindset is often required to embrace challenges with enthusiasm rather than doubt. It begins with the language you use. **Affirmations are a powerful tool in this regard**. By repeating statements of **courage and determination**, you rewire your brain to approach challenges positively. Instead of saying, "I can't handle this," try affirming, "**I am capable and will find a way through.**" This mental exercise **builds resilience, transforming fear into fuel for action**. Another technique is to visualize past successes when facing new challenges. Recall a time when you overcame a difficult situation and focus on the feelings of accomplishment and strength. These memories remind you of your ability to tackle whatever comes your way.

The unknown. Each challenge presents an opportunity to learn and adapt and encourages continuous improvement. Embracing the discomfort of growth fosters a mindset that welcomes challenges as opportunities. **With the right mindset and strategies, you transform obstacles into stepping stones, charting a path toward personal fulfillment and success.**

2.5 BUILDING RESILIENCE THROUGH LEARNING

Lifelong learning isn't just a motivational catchphrase—it's a practical strategy that nurtures resilience and cultivates a growth mindset. It's about actively choosing to grow every day, no matter where you are in life. Picture the vast expanse of knowledge available at your fingertips, from online courses to community workshops. Enrolling in these educational opportunities opens doors to new skills and ideas, keeping your mind agile and adaptable. Consider stepping outside your comfort zone by taking a course you wouldn't usually explore. This broadens your knowledge and builds the resilience to face new challenges head-on.

Whether learning a new language or mastering digital marketing, each new skill adds to your toolkit, making you more adaptable and resilient when facing life's inevitable changes and challenges.

Learning from others is another powerful avenue for growth. Biographies and stories of resilient figures offer invaluable lessons. When you read about individuals who have faced adversity and emerged victorious, you gain insights into the attitudes and strategies that fueled their perseverance. Consider the life of Helen Keller, who overcame the dual challenges of being deaf and blind to become a celebrated author and activist. **Her story, filled with determination and grit, is a testament to the human spirit's capacity to overcome even the most challenging obstacles.** By immersing yourself in such narratives, you cultivate a mindset that sees **challenges as opportunities for growth,** drawing inspiration from those who have walked similar paths.

Curiosity serves as the driving force behind lifelong learning. It compels you to ask "why" questions, probing beneath the surface to uncover a more profound understanding. This inquisitive outlook creates a learning culture where each day presents a chance to discover something new. Encourage yourself to question the world around you, seek out answers, and explore unfamiliar territories. This practice enhances your knowledge and builds resilience by providing the tools to navigate uncertainty. A curious mind remains open, adaptable, and ready to learn, regardless of the circumstances.

Applying new real-life skills is where the magic of learning truly manifests. It's not enough to simply acquire knowledge; you must actively put it into practice. For instance, a creative writing course is only valuable when you start writing your novel or submitting articles to a magazine, **you must put it into practice.** Imagine you've taken a course in creative writing. The real growth happens when you start writing that novel or contributing articles to a local magazine. Hands-on projects and real-world applications solidify your learning. They allow you to test theories, refine techniques, and receive valuable feedback, which in turn boosts your confidence and hones your skills. Whether through volunteer work, side projects, or professional implementations, applying what you've learned bridges the gap between theory and practice, fostering a deeper, more resilient understanding.

Interactive Element: Skills Application Worksheet

Start by listing the skills you've recently acquired or wish to develop. Beside each skill, write down potential real-life applications, such as projects or tasks, that you can practice and refine. Set a timeline for when you'll implement these applications. This exercise helps you plan to apply new knowledge and encourages accountability and follow-through. Taking action ensures that learning translates into tangible growth and personal development.

Resilience thrives on the foundation of continuous learning. **As you adopt the mindset of a lifelong learner, you build a reservoir of skills and knowledge that fortifies you against life's uncertainties and strengthens your emotional and mental resilience.** By actively seeking educational opportunities, learning from others, nurturing curiosity, and applying new skills, you cultivate a growth-oriented perspective that transforms challenges into stepping stones. This approach enhances personal growth and provides the adaptability and resilience needed to excel, personally and professionally, in today's fast-paced world. In this endeavor, **learning becomes an activity and a way of life that enriches your mind and empowers your spirit.**

2.6 CELEBRATING SMALL WINS

Imagine standing at the start of a long, winding trail. The destination is out of sight, obscured by the twists and turns ahead. At first glance, the journey seems highly challenging, but then you notice the markers along the path, small signs of progress that guide and encourage you. Recognizing progress and growth in your life is like spotting those markers on your journey—it gives you a sense of accomplishment and reinforces the idea that every step forward, no matter how small, is meaningful. No matter how insignificant, each small achievement is a testament to your efforts and dedication. **Daily reflection on your accomplishments, even the smallest ones, testifies how far you've come. This practice boosts** your morale and reinforces the realization that growth is a series of small steps, each building upon the last.

Consider the impact of creating a "win list." This simple tool involves noting every minor victory you achieve, whether completing a task, learning something new, or overcoming a moment of doubt. As you add to the list, it evolves into a tangible record of your growth, showcasing your resilience and reinforcing your capabilities. As you review these wins, you build momentum, each entry on the list propelling you forward. Over time, the cumulative effect of these small wins can shift your mindset and boost your confidence, making the impossible seem more achievable. **They transform your mindset, shifting your focus from what remains undone to what has been accomplished, instilling a sense of achievement that fuels further success.**

Positive reinforcement plays a vital role in sustaining motivation. y rewarding yourself for meeting milestones, you set up a positive feedback loop that keeps you motivated to keep going. Rewards don't have to be big; they can be as simple as taking a break, enjoying a favorite snack, or indulging in a hobby. The key is to truly recognize your progress and give yourself the credit you deserve for your hard work. This reinforcement makes the process enjoyable and strengthens your commitment to your goals. Knowing a reward is on the horizon gives you that extra push to power through challenges, reinforcing the belief that every ounce of effort is worth it.

Confidence is not built overnight; it grows incrementally with each small success. With each goal you achieve, no matter how small, you reinforce your ability to succeed and build the foundation for bigger wins. This gradual accumulation of successes builds a solid foundation of self-assurance. **Incremental goal setting** is an effective strategy for confidence building. By setting achievable targets, you create opportunities for consistent success. As you meet these goals, your confidence blossoms like a flower in full bloom, giving you the strength to tackle even bigger challenges. Building confidence through small wins **creates a positive cycle where success breeds more success.**

When combined, these practices—recognizing progress, celebrating small wins, using positive reinforcement, and building confidence incrementally—create a powerful approach to personal growth. Each small win becomes a stepping stone, not just leading you to greater achievements, but also strengthening the belief that you are capable of far more than you've ever imagined. As you embrace this mindset, you begin to see the bigger picture, where every effort counts and every step forward is a victory. With this perspective, **challenges become opportunities,** and setbacks are merely pauses on the path to success. The journey is ongoing, and each small win is a reminder that you are moving in the right direction. As we move forward, we turn our focus to nurturing connections with others, exploring how community and support can magnify our growth and resilience.

The Power of Growth:

I once stood young, with little to show,
No skills, no wealth, no place to go.
But in my heart, a spark held tight,
A drive to learn, to find my light.
Through trial and time, I came to see,
A growth mindset could set me free.

A fixed mind fears what change can bring,
It shrinks from risk, afraid to cling.
Yet growth reminds us skills can bloom,
Through work and time, we carve our room.
Each stumble forms a stepping stone,
With effort, strength becomes our own.

The brain's design is built to mold,
To stretch, to shift, to break the old.
With every challenge we embrace,
We forge new paths, we shape our space.
Neuroplasticity reveals,
That learning grows as passion fuels.

Failure, once feared, can teach us well,
A whispered guide, a tale to tell.
It's not the end, but lessons shared,
A chance to rise, a heart repaired.
Through trials faced and hope held near,
Resilience shines, defying fear.

The road ahead may twist and wind,
But with a vision, growth we find.
Through gratitude, we shift our view,
And challenges reveal what's true.
Each lesson learned, each dream pursued,
Transforms our world with fortitude.

So step by step, embrace the fight,
Each goal achieved, a guiding light.
Celebrate the small you gain,
For little wins will ease the strain.
In every trial, a chance anew,
The power of growth resides in you.

3

PRACTICAL STRATEGIES FOR OVERCOMING SELF-DOUBT

"Surrounded by a sea of applicants, a wave of insecurity crashed over me. The tall, beautiful people around me exuded an effortless confidence that made me feel small, their presence almost suffocating. At that moment, doubt crept in—how could I possibly distinguish myself in such a competitive selection process? Among the crowd, I was one of the shortest persons, a visible reminder that I was too ambitious to go there. We each received a number and were instructed to line up for the panel of interviewers to look at us. It felt less like a job interview and more like a beauty pageant, where I was certain I was not qualified. The interviewer coldly announced that only a few would make it to the next step—the dreaded panel interview. It meant that if the interviewers don't like how we look, we don't even have a chance for an interview. As the numbers were called, some instructed to step back and others to step forward, a doubtful whisper plastered into my thoughts: "You can't secure this job. You lack the maturity, the sophistication, the height. You can't possibly be a flight attendant."

3.1 IDENTIFYING AND CHALLENGING SELF-TALK

These words are from our inner critic—a relentless voice that scrutinizes every action, quick to judge and undermine our worth. Its language is negative self-talk, an ongoing stream of unspoken thoughts that can influence your self-esteem and perception of life. When unchecked, it can lead to a pessimistic mindset that clouds your view of the world. These thoughts often stem from past experiences, societal pressures, or personal insecurities, crafting a narrative that is all too easy to believe. **Understanding how this voice manifests is the first step toward silencing it, allowing you to reclaim your confidence and self-worth.**

Negative self-talk takes many forms, from small doubts to overwhelming fears, each with a subtle yet powerful impact. One such pattern is **catastrophizing**—the tendency to view every setback as a disaster waiting to happen. For example, a missed deadline at work can quickly escalate into fears of job loss and long-term career failure. This pattern magnifies problems, often clouding one's ability to focus on practical solutions and constructive steps forward.

Another typical pattern is **overgeneralization**, where one failure convinces you that you're destined to fail in similar situations. When you fumbled in a presentation, suddenly, you're convinced that public speaking is not for you. These patterns are irrational and detrimental, reinforcing a cycle of self-doubt that undermines your potential.

Challenging these negative thoughts requires consistent effort and proven cognitive techniques. One such method is the **"What evidence do I have?"** technique, a powerful tool for disputing irrational beliefs. When faced with a negative thought, pause and question its validity. For instance, if you think, 'I'm terrible at my job,' ask yourself, 'What actual proof supports this belief? Ask yourself if there's concrete evidence to support this belief or if it's merely a product of fear and insecurity. This process helps you separate fact from fiction, grounding your thoughts in reality rather than speculation. Another practical approach is reframing these thoughts with positive affirmations. Replace "I'll never succeed" with "I have the skills to improve and succeed." **Positive affirmations not only counteract negativity but also instill a sense of hope and possibility.**

Creating a positive inner dialogue is crucial for cultivating a supportive mindset. Daily affirmations actively challenge your inner critic, reinforcing your strengths and potential. Begin each day with affirmations that resonate with you, such as "I am capable" or "I am worthy of success." This practice **shifts your focus from limitations to possibilities, gradually transforming your mindset.** Equally important is practicing self-compassion—for instance, if you make a mistake, respond with the same understanding you'd give a close friend. **When you fail, remember that mistakes are part of being human and that there are opportunities to learn and grow. Embrace imperfection as a stepping stone rather than a stumbling block.**

Reflection Exercise: Identifying Your Inner Critic

Take a moment to reflect on recent instances of negative self-talk. Write down the specific thoughts and situations where your inner critic prevailed. Next, challenge these thoughts using the "What evidence do I have?" technique. Identify any patterns, such as catastrophizing or overgeneralization, and consider how you can reframe them with positive affirmations. Use this exercise to develop a supportive inner dialogue that encourages growth and resilience.

As you overcome self-doubt, remember that changing your inner dialogue is gradual. It requires **patience, practice, and persistence.** Understanding and challenging negative self-talk lays the foundation for a more confident and empowered self. As you cultivate a positive inner dialogue, you begin to see yourself not as a person with weak discretions but as a **reservoir of potential and strength, ready to face whatever challenges lie ahead.**

3.2 COGNITIVE-BEHAVIORAL TECHNIQUES FOR CONFIDENCE

Cognitive-behavioral therapy (CBT) is a transformative approach to overcoming self-doubt and building confidence. **At its core, CBT examines the intricate relationship between thoughts, feelings, and behaviors.** Imagine your mind as a complex web, where a single negative thought can ripple through, influencing your emotions and actions. When you believe "I'm not good enough," it can lead to feelings of inadequacy and avoidance of challenges, reinforcing the initial thought. CBT helps break this cycle by encouraging you to question and replace these beliefs with more empowering ones. By understanding how thoughts influence feelings and actions, you gain the power to change your mindset, experiences, and outcomes.

A key CBT technique is the **thought record exercise**, which helps analyze and reframe negative thinking patterns. The process begins with identifying automatic negative thoughts that arise in specific situations. For instance, if you're about to give a presentation and think, "I'll embarrass myself," jot it down. Next, examine the evidence for and against this thought. Is there concrete proof that you'll fail, or is this fear based on past experiences or unfounded assumptions? You gain clarity and perspective by dissecting these thoughts, allowing you to challenge and change them. Over time, this practice helps shift your mental landscape from one dominated by doubt to one full of confidence.

Behavioral experiments offer a hands-on approach to building confidence through action. These experiments involve trying new activities that challenge self-doubt, allowing you to test and adjust your beliefs. Consider taking up a hobby or skill that has always intrigued you but seemed difficult. Whether it's joining a dance class, learning a musical instrument, or volunteering for a leadership role, each new experience provides evidence that you are capable of growth and can learn to adapt. Engaging in social scenarios is another practical experiment. If you find social situations intimidating, start by attending small gatherings or networking events. As you navigate these interactions, you'll notice a gradual increase in your social confidence, reinforcing the belief that you can handle new environments and form connections.

Goal-setting within the CBT framework is an invaluable technique for cultivating confidence. Setting achievable, confidence-boosting goals provides a structured roadmap for personal growth. Short-term goals act as stepping stones toward larger objectives, providing a sense of achievement and momentum. Begin with small, manageable goals that align with your values and aspirations. If you struggle with public speaking, start by contributing a comment in a meeting or giving a brief presentation to a small group. As you accomplish these short-term goals, your confidence grows, preparing you for more ambitious challenges. This process builds confidence incrementally and instills a sense of purpose and direction in your journey of self-improvement.

Thought Record Template

Develop a straightforward template to structure your thought record exercises. Divide a sheet of paper into columns labeled **Situation, Automatic Thought, Evidence For, Evidence Against, and Alternative Thought**. Utilize this framework to document and analyze your thoughts, fostering a more balanced and confident mindset.

By integrating these CBT techniques into your daily life, you begin to see confidence as a skill that can be developed and strengthened. Every thought record, behavioral experiment, and goal-setting exercise contribute to dismantling self-doubt and establishing a strong foundation of self-assurance. **Through practice and persistence, you transform how you perceive yourself and your capabilities, fostering a mindset that embraces challenges and celebrates growth.**

3.3 VISUALIZATION FOR SUCCES

As discussed in the previous chapter, visualization shifts perspectives and serves as a practical tool for achieving success. Imagine standing at the starting line of a marathon. You've trained for months, but at this moment, it's not just physical readiness that counts. It's mental preparation that carries you forward. **Visualization is a mental rehearsal technique that transforms potential into performance—a strategy long used by athletes to enhance success.** Studies consistently show that athletes who practice visualization perform better as they mentally rehearse every step, every breath, and every victory, embedding success into their minds. This practice is not for athletes alone; it's a strategy you can use to boost confidence and clarity in everyday life.

To harness the power of visualization, begin by creating vivid mental images of your success. Picture yourself achieving a specific goal with as much detail as possible. If you're preparing for a job interview, imagine walking into the room, confidently shaking hands, and articulating your thoughts quickly. Feel the texture of the chair beneath you, the warmth of the room, and the calmness in your voice. Visualization becomes more potent when you incorporate all your senses, creating a comprehensive experience that the mind perceives as accurate. **This sensory engagement strengthens neural pathways, making success possible and inevitable.**

Consistency is key to effective visualization, so consider incorporating it into your daily routine. Set aside time each morning for a brief visualization session. Find a quiet space, close your eyes, and focus on your goals. Whether it's acing a presentation or launching a new project, visualize each step you'll take and the emotions you'll feel upon achieving it. These sessions ground you in your aspirations, setting a positive tone for the day ahead. **Over time, this practice builds confi-**

dence and motivation, reinforcing your belief in your ability to succeed.

Many successful individuals across various fields have shared the profound impact of visualization, proving its effectiveness as a transformative strategy. Entrepreneurs often use visualization to map out business strategies and lead to success. Picture a tech startup founder visualizing the launch of a groundbreaking app. As she envisions each stage of development and the satisfying emotion at its launch, she mentally prepares for the challenges and celebrations. This mental rehearsal guides her actions, instilling confidence and ensuring preparedness for real-world scenarios. **Visualization isn't merely a daydream; it's a catalyst for transformation, turning aspirations into tangible achievements.**

Real-life examples illustrate the transformative power of visualization. Consider the story of a musician who uses visualization before stepping onto the concert stage. He imagines the applause, the spotlight's warmth, and the music flowing effortlessly from his fingers. This mental practice calms his nerves and sharpens his focus, transforming anxiety into anticipation. As he takes the stage, the visualization serves as a mental map, guiding him through each note with confidence and poise. **Visualization empowers you to walk past your limitations, transforming uncertainty into a roadmap for success.**

When applied consistently, visualization becomes a cornerstone of personal growth. It bridges the gap between intention and action, making us see our goals and the path to make them happen. By vividly and consistently imagining your success, you align your thoughts, emotions, and actions, creating the way for real-world achievements. **The mind is a powerful tool; training it to see success sets the stage for it to unfold in reality.**

3.4 SETTING AND ACHIEVING PERSONAL GOALS

Setting goals is like plotting a course on a map. It directs you, ensuring that the trail you take leads you toward your destination. When you set goals, you're not just outlining aspirations but creating a tangible path to follow. **This clarity bolsters self-assurance.** Knowing where you're headed allows you to measure progress and celebrate milestones. **Goals act as motivators, providing benchmarks for success and a sense of accomplishment as each is reached.** They turn abstract dreams into concrete plans, giving you the confidence to achieve what you set your mind to.

Breaking down goals into smaller, manageable steps bridges intention and execution. Significant goals can seem daunting but become achievable when deconstructed into smaller tasks. Start by creating a detailed task list with timelines for each step. If your goal is to write a book, start by crafting an outline, then establish deadlines for each chapter. This approach provides a clear roadmap and enhances motivation. Each completed task serves as a milestone, propelling you toward your larger goal. Focusing on one step at a time, you maintain momentum and prevent overwhelm, ensuring consistent progress.

Interactive Goal-Setting Exercise

Take a moment to identify a personal goal you wish to achieve. Use the SMART framework—ensuring your goal is Specific, Measurable, Achievable, Relevant, and Time-bound—to refine it with clear definitions. Next, break down the goal into actionable steps, creating a task list with timelines. Use a journal or app to track your progress, noting achievements and any adjustments needed. By completing this exercise, you gain clarity on your objectives and create a structured approach to achieving them, reinforcing the belief that every goal is attainable.

As you embrace the practice of goal setting, you discover its transformative power. Each goal becomes a stepping stone, guiding you toward greater self-assurance and fulfillment. **By setting, pursuing, and achieving personal goals, you cultivate a sense of purpose and direction, reinforcing the reality that you have the power to shape your future.** Through this practice, you build a path to success and the confidence to walk it with determination and resilience.

3.5 MASTERING POSITIVE SELF-REINFORCEMENT

> "I finished consulting a group of temporary foreign workers. They asked questions on almost every subject, both imaginary and tangible—questions that stretched my skills and tested my patience. I felt a sense of accomplishment in the quiet moment that followed when I was alone at my office. I knew I made a difference in their chaotic moments. I settled their confusion and gave them the correct direction to follow. It was a calming moment."

This is where positive reinforcement comes into play—acknowledging and rewarding yourself for accomplishments, both big and small. Positive reinforcement acts as a stimulus for confidence, encouraging you to tackle future problems enthusiastically. **By rewarding yourself, you celebrate success and reinforce the behaviors that led to it. This cycle of achievement and reward creates momentum that propels you forward, building a foundation of confidence that grows stronger with each accomplishment.**

To harness the power of positive reinforcement, create a personal reward system tailored to your preferences. This system could be as simple or elaborate as you want. Start by identifying what you find rewarding—perhaps it's a favorite treat, a foot massage, or a new book. Assign these rewards to specific achievements or milestones. For example, completing a week of consistent workouts might earn you a relaxing spa day. This approach motivates you to achieve your goals and adds a layer of enjoyment to the process.

Another technique is to **engage in positive self-talk** after accomplishing tasks. Take a moment to acknowledge your effort and remind yourself of the skills and determination that brought you to this point. **This practice reinforces a positive self-image, gradually replacing doubt with confidence.**

Developing a structured plan for self-reinforcement is essential for maintaining consistency. Begin by planning small rewards for small victories.

These rewards serve as immediate gratification, reinforcing the positive behaviors that lead to success. For more considerable achievements, prepare more significant rewards that reflect the effort involved. The key is to ensure the rewards are meaningful to you and proportionate to the accomplishment. This **structured approach** keeps you motivated and ensures that reinforcement remains a part of your routine. By planning rewards, you create a roadmap that guides your actions, inspiring you to stay focused and committed to your goals.

The impact of reinforcement on long-term confidence growth is profound. **Consistent reinforcement** helps solidify positive habits, turning them into second nature. Consider the example of habit formation through reinforcement. Imagine you set a goal to read a new book each month. Imagine setting a goal to read one book per month. Each time you finish, you treat yourself to a relaxing afternoon at your favorite café, enjoying a delicious pastry. Over time, the association between reading and the reward strengthens, making the habit more ingrained and enjoyable. The same principle applies to **confidence-building behaviors.** By consistently reinforcing these behaviors, you create a cycle of success and reward that fuels your confidence. As this cycle continues, your self-assurance grows, becoming an integral part of your character.

Incorporating positive reinforcement into your life is more than just a strategy for achieving goals. It's a mindset shift that celebrates progress and acknowledges effort. As you practice self-reinforcement, you cultivate a sense of pride in your accomplishments, no matter how small they may seem. This practice empowers you to approach challenges with renewed purpose and determination. With each reward, you reinforce the belief that you can achieve greatness and that success is a journey of many small victories. In this way, **positive reinforcement becomes a tool for building confidence and a life filled with purpose, joy, and fulfillment.**

3.6 BUILDING CONFIDENCE THROUGH COMPETENCE

The confidence you feel isn't just the result of positive thinking—it's the natural outcome of competence, built through preparation and mastery of your subject. The confidence you feel isn't just a result of positive thinking—it's the natural outcome of competence, the assurance born from knowing your subject inside and out. Developing skills and competencies is a powerful way to bolster confidence because it provides a foundation of self-assurance that can't be easily shaken. **When you know what you're doing, you move with certainty and speak with authority. This inner knowledge is your strength, ensuring you can rely on your expertise despite uncertainty.**

Identifying areas for skill development is the first step. Start by reflecting on your strengths and the areas where growth would enhance your confidence. Take a moment to reflect on what you wish to improve, whether in your personal or professional life. Consider where your interests lie and what skills could enhance your capabilities. Perhaps there's a gap in your professional skill set you wish to fill or a personal hobby you've always wanted to explore more deeply. Assessing these gaps involves both introspection and feedback from those around you. Ask colleagues or friends for their perspective on your strengths and areas for growth. This feedback can provide valuable insights, helping you prioritize which skills to focus on.

Once you have a clear idea of the skills you wish to develop, **the next step is to acquire them effectively.** Enrolling in relevant courses or workshops is a practical method for gaining new knowledge and honing existing skills. Many educational resources, both in-person and online, cater to various interests and expertise levels. Choose programs that align with your goals and offer hands-on experience. Another invaluable resource is seeking **mentorship** from those more experienced in your field. A mentor can provide professional guidance, share applicable insights, and offer constructive feedback, accelerating your learning process and helping you avoid common pitfalls.

Demonstrating competence in real-world scenarios is crucial for building confidence. This action involves applying newly acquired skills in practical settings where the stakes are real and the outcomes matter. Whether taking on a challenging project at work, leading a community initiative, or simply practicing a new hobby, putting your skills to the test is where actual growth happens. These experiences reinforce your abilities and provide a platform to showcase your competencies to others. **Each time** you successfully apply your skills, your confidence grows, reinforcing your belief in your capabilities and inspiring you to take on greater challenges.

As we conclude this chapter on overcoming self-doubt, it's clear that **building confidence is an active process**, one that involves nurturing competence and applying it in real-world contexts. Remember, every skill you develop adds a layer to your foundation of confidence. **With each new competency, you become more equipped to face life's challenges.** As we move forward, we'll explore how to navigate life's transitions with courage, further building upon the resilience and confidence you've begun to cultivate.

Breaking Through Doubt:

I stood among the towering crowd,
Self-doubt within me spoke so loud.
Their poise, their grace, their height, their style,
I shrank inside, my thoughts ran wild.
But deep within, a voice broke through,
"You are enough. This is for you."

The critic whispers tales of fear,
A voice that mocks what we hold dear.
It paints our flaws, it fuels despair,
Yet truth lies waiting if we dare.
We challenge doubt, we shift the frame,
Rewriting thoughts to fuel our flame.

With every thought, a choice is made,
To rise above or shrink and fade.
Through mindful steps, through careful phrase,
We craft a brighter, bolder gaze.
Affirm the strength, embrace the fight,
Reclaim your voice, reclaim your light.

Success begins within the mind,
Where vivid dreams and goals aligned.
Visualize each step ahead,
And walk the path your heart has led.
With eyes on hope and fears aside,
You'll find the strength you hold inside.

Step by step, the climb feels real,
Each small win builds the strength you feel.
Set your goals and mark your way,
Let discipline define your stay.
In every task, in every stride,
You shape the power found inside.

Confidence grows where effort stays,
Through skill and practice, steady days.
Embrace the work, refine your art,
Each lesson learned, a stronger heart.
For competence will pave the way,
And self-belief will always stay.

4

NAVIGATING LIFE TRANSITIONS WITH COURAGE

Transitioning from student life to a full-time job pushed me into a phase of forced growth. The challenge ahead was not just a change in routine but a test of my resilience and courage. The most daunting part of my training was

a survival swimming course with critical safety requirements. This course required every new hire, including me, to dive into deep waters, tread for 45 minutes, escape from underwater holds, rescue a peer, and cross an Olympic-sized pool. My obstacle? I had never learned to swim. Determined to overcome this hurdle, I mentally prepared myself for the challenge. Seeking help, I asked a cousin, who offered his spare time to teach me the basics of swimming, and I practiced and practiced by myself. Despite his guidance, as the test day approached, fear and doubt reminded me of my inexperience in the water. Yet, when faced with the pool's depths, something remarkable happened. Despite the fear gnawing at my confidence, I found a well of inner strength I hadn't known existed. Each stroke was a testament to my determination; every breath was a victory over self-doubt. Surprisingly, I completed the course, treading through the water with a resilience that carried me through the rest of the training module. This experience served not only as a lesson in swimming but as a profound reminder that courage often lies on the other side of fear, waiting to be discovered.

4.1 EMBRACING CHANGE AND UNCERTAINTY

This moment encapsulates the essence of life transitions, where change comes with both promise and uncertainty. **Change** is a constant force in our lives, shaping our days and defining our journeys. From ancient civilizations to the modern era, societies have demonstrated that embracing change is key to prosperity. Those who adapt survive and thrive by viewing change as an opportunity for innovation and growth rather than a threat. Embracing change is not just a necessity; it's a powerful motivator that can inspire you to reach new heights.

The newly introduced concept of '**collective adaptation**' provides a framework for understanding how human communities evolve in response to changing circumstances, emphasizing adaptation's crucial role in building societal resilience. However, the human mind naturally seeks certainty and often perceives the unknown with fear. While uncertainty can easily be associated with fear, adopting a different perspective can create opportunities for growth and discovery.

Uncertainty is not a void to be feared; it is a canvas waiting for possibilities. Consider the story of Estee Lauder, a company that found success amidst the uncertainty of a global pandemic by leveraging customer data to adapt and innovate, ensuring continued engagement with its audience. This development wasn't planned from certainty but from a willingness to explore new strategies. Such stories serve as reminders that **within the folds of uncertainty lie the seeds of opportunity.**

Developing comfort with the unknown requires practice and resilience. One effective technique is to **visualize scenarios** where you successfully navigate unexpected challenges. Picture yourself faced with a difficult situation at work. Rather than feeling overwhelmed, imagine calmly evaluating your options and devising a solution. This exercise strengthens your mental agility, preparing you to face the unknown confidently. Another approach involves **creating practice scenarios** for dealing with unexpected events. Think of a day when a sudden change in plans disrupts your routine. Use this as an opportunity to practice adaptability, focusing on finding creative solutions rather than succumbing to stress. Each practice session builds your resilience, equipping you to handle real-life uncertainties gracefully. Remember, **resilience is not just about bouncing back; it's about thriving in the face of change feeling empowered and capable.**

Reframing fear of change into excitement for new possibilities is a powerful mindset shift. Rather than viewing change as a loss of control, see it as an **invitation to evolve.** This shift begins with the language you use. Instead of saying, "I fear what might happen," try reframing it to, "I'm excited to see what unfolds." This subtle change transforms apprehension into anticipation, opening your mind to potential opportunities. Another technique is to **focus on the positive outcomes that change can bring.** Picture the new skills, experiences, and perspectives that await you on the other side of change. **By focusing on the potential benefits, you shift your mindset. This cultivates excitement that outweighs fear, pushing you forward with courage and optimism.** Remember, change is not just about the unknown; it's about the potential for growth and new experiences.

Reflection Section: Embracing Change

Take a moment to reflect on a recent change or transition in your life. Write down the emotions you felt and the challenges you faced. Now, consider the opportunities from this change and how you adapted. Use this reflection to identify areas where you can shift your mindset, viewing future changes as opportunities for growth. This exercise not only enhances your resilience but also prepares you to embrace the unknown with confidence.

Embracing change and uncertainty is not about eliminating fear but transforming it into a driver for growth. By understanding the nature of change, shifting your mindset, and developing comfort with the unknown, you can navigate life's transitions with courage and confidence. **Change becomes a bridge to new possibilities, guiding you toward a future rich with potential.**

4.2 FRAMEWORKS FOR DECISION-MAKING IN TRANSITIONS

Life transitions, be it a career change or a significant personal decision, often demand a structured approach to decision-making. When faced with numerous possibilities, frameworks can serve as invaluable tools to guide us toward sound choices. One such method is the **pros and cons analysis**, a simple way to weigh the advantages and disadvantages of each option. Listing the positives and negatives gives you a clearer picture of the potential outcomes. This method helps you visualize the balance between benefits and drawbacks, making a more informed decision.

Another helpful framework is **cost-benefit analysis**, which requires a more analytical approach. This method quantifies the benefits and costs of each decision, providing a numerical value that can guide your choices. By assigning a value to each factor, you gain a more objective perspective, allowing for a practical evaluation of your options. This approach is beneficial for decisions that involve financial or resource-based considerations, where the stakes are high, and clarity is essential.

Evaluating options and outcomes can become complex, especially when dealing with significant transitions. **Decision trees** offer a visual representation of choices and potential consequences. By mapping out each possible path, you can see the ripple effects of each decision, helping you anticipate outcomes and prepare for alternative plans. This method is beneficial when scenarios are complex, providing a clear roadmap of possibilities. **Scenario planning** is another technique that involves envisioning different futures based on your choices. By considering various scenarios, you gain insights into the long-term implications of your decisions, allowing you to handle unexpected developments with more remarkable foresight.

Incorporating values into decision-making is crucial for aligning choices with personal beliefs and priorities. What values guide your biggest decisions? What are your non-negotiable? Consider what truly matters to you, whether it be integrity, family, or personal growth. By **understanding your values, you can ensure that your decisions reflect your authentic self, leading to greater satisfaction and fulfillment.** This alignment acts as a compass, guiding you through transitions with a sense of purpose and conviction.

Reflecting on past decisions offers valuable lessons for future choices. Take time to analyze previous transitions, examining what worked well and what could have been improved. This reflection provides a rich source of insights, highlighting patterns and tendencies that may influence current decisions. By learning from past experiences, you gain wisdom and perspective, enabling you to navigate future transitions more confidently and clearly.

Interactive Element: Core Values Exercise

Take a moment to write down your core values. What motivates you when faced with tough choices? What non-negotiable do you stand by? Use this list to evaluate current and future choices, ensuring they align with your true self. This exercise clarifies your values and strengthens your decision-making process, providing a foundation for choices that resonate with your beliefs.

Decision-making during transitions is not merely about choosing the right path but about understanding the implications and aligning them with your values. By utilizing frameworks like pros and cons, cost-benefit analysis, decision trees, and scenario planning, you arm yourself with the tools to navigate complex transitions. Incorporating your core values ensures that your choices reflect your authentic self, leading to more fulfilling outcomes. **Reflecting on past decisions enriches this process, offering lessons that guide you toward a future that honors your true self.**

4.3 CREATING ADAPTABLE PLANS FOR CHANGE

What happens when a well-established business faces a sudden market shift? The most successful companies thrive by embracing flexibility and adapting their strategies to meet new realities. **Flexibility is a necessity in navigating life's transitions.** It allows for adjustments without derailing progress. This adaptability is evident in businesses like Vyaire Medical, which increased production and met soaring demands by modernizing their data systems during the pandemic. Their ability to pivot highlights the power of flexible planning—showing how preparation and adaptability turn challenges into opportunities, a principle equally valuable in personal transitions.

Developing **contingency plans** is like having a safety net while walking a tightrope—it ensures stability when unexpected challenges arise. Begin by identifying potential risks and evaluating possible outcomes. This proactive approach helps you create structured backup plans to navigate various challenges effectively. Taking this proactive approach enables you to create well-structured backup plans designed to address a range of scenarios. A personal contingency plan template might include **listing resources, alternative strategies, and support networks you can rely on.** If you're planning a career change, your contingency plan might include updating your resume, exploring freelance opportunities, and networking with professionals in your field. What steps can you take today to prepare for an unexpected shift? These preparations ensure you're not caught off guard when the unexpected occurs but instead prepared to navigate the challenges confidently.

Setting both short- and long-term goals is essential for navigating change with intention. Short-term goals act as stepping stones, providing immediate targets and a sense of accomplishment, while long-term goals offer a vision for the future. Goal-setting workshops offer real-life examples and peer support, helping you refine your objectives and stay committed to achieving them. In these workshops, you might encounter individuals who set a short-term goal to complete a certification course with a long-term goal of transitioning to a new career.

Adapting plans is an ongoing process—life rarely follows a fixed path, so regular reflection and flexibility are key. Life rarely unfolds as planned, and being open to changing your course is crucial. Regularly review your progress and reflect on what's working and what isn't. This reflection allows you to refine your approach, ensuring alignment with your changing circumstances and goals. Tools like calendars, journals, or digital apps can help you track progress, offering a visual reminder of how far you've come and where adjustments are needed. These tools provide visual feedback, showing how far you've come and where you must turn. By remaining open to change and willing to adjust plans, you maintain momentum and resilience, even when faced with unexpected challenges.

As discussed in previous chapters, a real-life exercise that complements these strategies involves creating a **vision board**. This visual reminder motivates you and keeps your goals at the forefront of your mind, guiding your actions and decisions. ach milestone is a step forward—update your vision board to celebrate progress and refine aspirations. This practice reminds you that while plans may evolve, your ultimate vision remains steadfast.

In cultivating adaptable plans for change, you prepare yourself with the tools to navigate life's uncertainties with confidence and clarity. Embrace flexibility, create contingency plans, set strategic goals, and remain open to adjustments. **These practices form the foundation of resilience, empowering you to face transitions with courage and optimism.**

4.4 MANAGING STRESS IN TRANSITIONAL PHASES

Transitions in life often bring a mix of emotions, with stress being a common and sometimes overwhelming presence. Identifying everyday stressors during these times is a valuable first step in managing them effectively. Whether it's starting a new job, relocating, or experiencing a significant personal change, life transitions bring a range of challenges that can feel overwhelming. Research highlights that uncertainty, financial strain, and disrupted routines are among the most common stressors during life transitions. **Understanding these everyday stressors helps you identify them, allowing you to tackle them with targeted strategies and clarity.**

Practical techniques for managing stress effectively during transitions are essential tools in your arsenal. **Mindful breathing exercises** offer a simple yet effective way to calm the mind and reduce stress. Take a moment to sit quietly, close your eyes, and focus on your breath. Inhale deeply through your nose, hold for a count of four, then exhale slowly through your mouth. This rhythmic breathing helps lower your heart rate and alleviate anxiety, grounding you in the present moment. **Progressive muscle relaxation routines** also provide relief by systematically tensing and relaxing muscle groups. Start from your toes and work your way up, releasing tension and inviting relaxation into your body. More than mere techniques, these exercises serve as lifelines, providing comfort during uncertainty.

Building a stress resilience toolkit equips you to face challenges confidently and calmly. Consider incorporating **meditation apps** into your daily routine, offering guided sessions tailored to your needs. These apps provide structure and support, making meditation accessible even on the busiest days. In addition, transcribing your thoughts may alleviate stress. **Journaling** helps process emotions and offers perspective, making challenges feel more manageable. Set aside time each day to jot down your thoughts, fears, and hopes. This practice not only releases pent-up stress but also fosters self-reflection and clarity. As you build your toolkit, remember that it is uniquely yours, filled with resources that resonate with you and your lifestyle.

The role of **support systems** in managing stress cannot be overstated. Friends, family, and professionals offer a network of support that bolsters your resilience. Reaching out to loved ones provides a sense of belonging and reassurance, reminding you that **you are not alone in your strug-**

gles. Consider seeking professional guidance, whether a therapist, coach, or counselor. These individuals offer valuable insights and strategies tailored to your situation, empowering you to navigate transitions more easily.

Strong support systems offer both comfort and guidance, reinforcing the power of human connection. While we may feel isolated in our vulnerabilities and uncertainties, it's crucial to remember that support is available if we seek it out. Often, those around us may be unaware of our struggles or hesitant to intervene, unsure how we will receive their assistance. Recognizing this, it becomes clear that reaching out is not just an act of seeking help but also an invitation for connection, **reminding us that we are not alone. Many hands are ready to lift us—we only need to reach out to them.**

Patience is frequently praised but often overlooked in today's fast-paced world. However, during times of change, it becomes an essential asset. **It enables us to navigate uncertainty with composure, helping to avoid impulsive decisions and unnecessary stress.** Patience provides the steady guidance needed to manage transitions effectively, offering the perspective to move beyond immediate challenges. Entrepreneur Alex Hormozi redefines patience as channeling focus into productive activities while waiting for long-term goals to materialize.

Most of us know the story of Colonel Harland Sanders, who exemplifies the power of patience. At 65, **Colonel Harland Sanders** encountered countless rejections while promoting his fried chicken recipe. Yet, his unwavering patience led to the birth of Kentucky Fried Chicken (KFC), now a global fast-food empire. The colonel's unwavering patience, facing rejections while trying to sell his fried chicken, became a cornerstone of his motivation, allowing him to emerge stronger after each rejection. **This patience wasn't passive waiting but active endurance, a commitment to a larger purpose despite the prolonged uncertainty.** Colonel's story teaches us that patience isn't about enduring without action but continuously moving towards your goal, even if it doesn't seem reachable.

Developing patience is a skill that can be cultivated through practice. One effective method is **mindfulness meditation, which focuses on** patience. This practice involves sitting quietly, observing your thoughts and feelings without judgment, and allowing them to pass without acting upon them. Begin by setting aside a few minutes each day to practice. As thoughts arise, acknowledge them and let them drift away like clouds across the sky. This exercise trains your mind to be present, reducing the urgency to react to every impulse. Over time, you develop a greater sense of calm and patience, extending this practice from meditation to daily life. Another exercise is the **patience jar**. Each time impatience arises, drop a coin into a jar. Over time, this tangible practice serves as a reminder of growth, encouraging reflection on triggers and lessons learned. This tangible practice serves as a reminder of your progress, fostering a mindset of patience.

Conversely, persistence is the driving force that keeps us moving forward, even when progress seems elusive. It propels us to get back up after a setback, dust ourselves off, and try again. **Setbacks are not failures but stepping stones, opportunities to learn and grow.** Consider the story of Thomas Edison, who, after thousands of failed attempts, finally succeeded in inventing the light bulb. Edison's persistence was fueled by his belief that **each failure brought him one step closer to success.** He famously said, "**I have not failed. I've just found 10,000 ways that won't work.**" Reframing setbacks as part of the discovery process illustrates how persistence can lead to breakthrough success. By viewing setbacks as stepping stones, you build resilience and gain invaluable lessons that bring you closer to success.

Fostering persistence in others begins with empathy and unwavering support. When a friend or loved one faces challenges, offer encouragement and remind them of past successes. Share stories of individuals who persevered through adversity, highlighting the qualities that led to their success. Help them see setbacks as stepping stones rather than roadblocks, shaping their journey rather than defining it. A supportive environment fuels persistence, creating a powerful ripple effect that strengthens not just one person but an entire community of resilience and determination. Providing a listening ear and offering constructive feedback can empower others to see their potential and continue striving toward their goals. Remind them that **persistence is not about never stumbling but about rising each time they do.**

Blending patience and persistence into your mindset reshapes how you navigate life's transitions. Together, they form a powerful duo, guiding you through transitions with grace and determination. **Patience offers the space to breathe and reflect, while persistence fuels the drive to continue moving forward.** The more you nurture patience and persistence, the more unshakable you become in the face of adversity.

4.5 FINDING OPPORTUNITY IN NEW BEGINNINGS

> *"Stepping into my flight attendant uniform, the snug skirt and three-inch heels felt both foreign and formidable. I whispered to myself, 'I can do this. I can walk through airports in these heels, uncomfortable as they are.' The gold wings pinned to my chest have my name, symbolizing readiness. Readiness to fly, readiness to embrace what this job demanded. This path wasn't one I had envisioned for myself. My dreams had been different; I had aspirations of finishing school and making a name for myself. Yet life's curveballs redirected me to this role, one I never saw coming. Despite the setback, I recognized it as a chance for learning, all for my family's sake. Flying wasn't just a job but an opportunity to start anew."*

The prospect of new beginnings often stirs a mix of excitement and apprehension. It's like standing at the edge of a vast, uncharted landscape, where every step holds potential for discovery. Viewing these beginnings as opportunities for growth and exploration can transform your perspective, turning uncertainty into a canvas for new experiences.

Consider the story of a (woman) who, after years in a stable career, decided to pursue a passion for writing. Initially daunting, this shift opened doors to unexpected opportunities and immense personal growth. Her journey shows how embracing new beginnings can lead to success, as she found fulfillment in transcribing her thoughts in words. Researching a topic she's writing about stirs her curiosity and fills her mind with new information she never knew before.

Personal anecdotes like these remind us that **new paths often lead to enriching experiences.**

Spotting opportunities amidst transitions requires a shift in focus from what is lost to what can be gained. One effective strategy is to engage in opportunity brainstorming sessions. Set aside time to jot down potential opportunities a current transition might bring. Whether learning a new skill, meeting new people, or exploring a different industry, this exercise helps you identify and prioritize possibilities that align with your goals. By focusing on what can be gained, you cultivate a mindset that sees transitions not as disruptions but as gateways to new adventures. This proactive approach empowers you to navigate change with optimism and clarity, ready to seize opportunities.

Transitions also provide fertile ground for developing and leveraging new skills. Use this time as a chance to enhance your abilities through skill-building workshops. These can range from online courses to community classes, where you can acquire new knowledge and refine existing skills. For instance, during a career change, attending workshops on leadership or digital marketing can train you with valuable tools for success in your new role. Networking opportunities during periods of change are equally important. Attend industry events, join professional groups, and connect with individuals who share your interests. These interactions expand your network and offer insights and inspiration, helping you navigate your transition with confidence and foresight.

Celebrating new beginnings is key to embracing change with open arms. **It marks the start of a new chapter, infusing it with positivity and excitement.** Consider organizing a small gathering with friends or family to commemorate the change. Share your hopes and aspirations, inviting their support and encouragement. This act of celebration becomes a powerful affirmation of your commitment to your new path. Another way to celebrate is through personal reflection. Reflect on the courage it took to embrace change and the endless potential it holds. **This reflection boosts your confidence and solidifies your resolve to pursue your new beginning with enthusiasm and determination.**

Transitions, though challenging, offer a wealth of opportunities for growth and development. You unlock a world of potential by reframing new beginnings as opportunities for exploration, identifying opportunities, leveraging new skills, and celebrating these changes. These practices empower you to approach transitions confidently, ready to embrace whatever comes next.

As we wrap up this chapter, remember that new beginnings are more than just changes; **they are disguised opportunities.** By embracing them, you open yourself to a world of growth and discovery. Now, as we move forward, let's explore the role of community in building resilience and strength.

Navigating Change with Courage:

I stepped into the waters deep,
My heart was racing, fears did creep.
A challenge vast, a test so grand,
With courage held within my hand.
Each stroke, each breath, a battle won,
The strength I found had just begun.

In life, the winds of change will blow,
Through highs and lows, through fast and slow.
The unknown whispers fear and doubt,
Yet growth is what it's all about.
When change arrives, don't turn away,
Embrace the chance to learn, to stay.

Decisions shape the paths we take,
With careful thought, the risks we break.
We weigh the costs, the gains we seek,
A forward step, both strong and meek.
Our values guide, our hearts hold true,
Through every choice, we start anew.

Adapt we must, with plans in place,
Prepared to shift, adjust our pace.
Contingency, our shield and guide,
Through setbacks faced, we turn with pride.
With goals in sight, both short and long,
Flexibility keeps us strong.

Transitions bring a touch of strain,
Yet patience soothes the sharpest pain.
Through breathing deep, through steady grace,
We find our strength, our rightful place.
With every trial, resilience grows,
A steady heart through highs and lows.

New starts are gifts wrapped up in time,
A chance to reach, to learn, to climb.
Embrace the fresh, the unknown wide,
With hope and courage side by side.
Each journey brings a world so bright,
A future shaped by inner light.

THE POWER OF SHARING YOUR STORY

"The best way to find yourself is to lose yourself in the service of others."

— MAHATMA GANDHI

When we lift others up, we grow stronger ourselves. Your words have the power to help someone who feels lost, uncertain, or alone.

Would you help someone just like you—searching for strength, hope, and resilience—but unsure where to start?

My mission is to make **emotional courage** and **inner strength** something real and attainable for everyone who needs it. But to reach more people, I need your help.

Most people choose books based on reviews. That means your voice matters. Your review could be a **sign someone is looking for** the encouragement they need to take the first step toward rebuilding their strength.

It costs nothing, takes less than a minute, and could change someone's journey. Your review could help…

- …someone facing loss finds hope.
- …someone struggling with self-doubt believes in themselves again.
- …someone searching for resilience discovers the strength they already have.
- …someone on the edge of giving up chooses to keep going.

Leave Your Review & Inspire Someone Today

To make a difference, simply **scan the QR code below** or click here to leave a review:

If this book helped you, your words could **be the start of someone else's desire to transform their lives for the better or learn how to carry their unbearable loads.**

Thank you from the bottom of my heart. Your kindness and generosity mean the world to me.

With my sincerest gratitude,
Arlene Grace Evangelista

5

BUILDING A SUPPORTIVE COMMUNITY

As I embarked on my journey into the skies, I discovered a few new friendships. Though few in number, these friendships were deeply cherished and profoundly meaningful. These new relationships marked a meaningful beginning for someone who has always been more reserved.

I began my journey with the belief that **'When all you have is you**, you must find strength within. Back then, I didn't realize there was a community because I didn't find one. As a young person, I never shared the agonizing pain that tore through me. I never felt comforted, never belonged to a group, and never knew where to find one. But it's not too late for you and me. There are many supportive groups, especially now. In this digital world, reaching out and finding the valuable connection we all need is not too difficult.

5.1 THE POWER OF CONNECTION

Imagine walking into a room filled with familiar faces. Each smile and nod acknowledges your presence, creating a comforting sense of belonging. The power of connection brings about this emotion. As humans, we are wired to seek bonds that bring comfort and security. These connections are more than just pleasant interactions; they are fundamental to our emotional well-being and personal growth. Research confirms that strong social ties improve mental health, easing symptoms of depression and anxiety. The hormone oxytocin, often called the "love hormone," plays a crucial role in this. It is released during positive social interactions and fosters bonding and trust. This biological response highlights the fundamental role that meaningful connections play in our lives.

A supportive community acts as a safety net, catching you when life feels overwhelming. Emotional support from friends, family, or even colleagues can provide comfort and guidance during crises. Knowing someone is there to listen and offer a shoulder to lean on can make all the difference. In addition to emotional rescue, strong social networks open doors to numerous opportunities. Networking is a powerful tool for career advancement, as connections often lead to new prospects and collaborations. When you engage with a diverse group of people, you gain access to a wealth of knowledge and resources, enhancing your resilience and adaptability in various situations. More than mere transactions, these interactions weave the fabric of a thriving, supportive community.

Recognizing who forms the core of your support system is not just important, it's vital. Your **family, friends, mentors, and colleagues** each play unique roles in your life. **Family** provides unconditional love and a foundation of values. **Friends** offer companionship and shared experiences that enrich your journey. **Mentors** guide you with their wisdom and knowledge, helping you navigate complex decisions. **Colleagues**, too, contribute to your professional growth, offering insights and collaboration. Identifying these key connections enables you to appreciate their significance and cultivate relationships that support your well-being and aspirations. By acknowledging the importance of these individuals, you create a diverse network capable of providing support in various aspects of life.

Forging new connections may feel daunting, but it is crucial for expanding your social network. Take the first step by venturing beyond your comfort zone and immersing yourself in new environments. These settings offer opportunities to meet like-minded individuals who share your values and goals. In today's digital world, online communities and forums provide valuable opportunities to connect with people who share your interests. Platforms focused on specific hobbies or professional fields allow you to connect with people worldwide, broadening your perspective and introducing you to new ideas. Remember, every connection starts with a simple conversation. **When you approach new encounters with openness and genuine curiosity, you'll discover that building relationships is both fulfilling and enriching**

Reflection Section: Mapping Your Support System

Pause for a moment to reflect on the meaningful connections in your life. Visualize your support system by mapping or listing the people in your life, categorizing them as family, friends, mentors, or colleagues. Consider how each person contributes to your well-being and growth. Pinpoint areas where you can strengthen existing connections or cultivate new ones. This exercise helps you analyze your current support system and highlights opportunities for building new connections. Through this process, you gain clarity on your most meaningful relationships and uncover ways to strengthen and nurture them.

Connection has the power to transform isolation into a community, offering both security and opportunity. As you cultivate and expand your social network, you enrich your own life and contribute to the collective resilience and growth of those around you. This transformation is a possibility and a reality waiting to be embraced.

5.2 BUILDING AND NURTURING RELATIONSHIPS

Strong relationships are the anchors that help us weather life's storms—built on the unwavering pillars of trust, communication, and empathy. **Trust is the cornerstone, fostering a sense of safety and openness.** Without trust, relationships falter as suspicion and doubt erode the bonds that hold us together. Building trust requires consistency and integrity—doing what you say and saying what you mean, even in the smallest moments.

Communication is the bridge that connects hearts and minds, creating pathways for understanding and collaboration. It involves more than just exchanging words; it's about **sharing thoughts, feelings, and experiences.** When we communicate openly and honestly, it paves the way for transparency and understanding, significantly reducing the risk of misinterpretation. **Empathy, the ability to understand and share the feelings of another, deepens these connections.** It lets you step into someone else's shoes, offering genuine support and compassion. **Active listening** is the cornerstone of empathy. It involves focusing fully on the speaker, acknowledging their emotions, and responding in a way that shows you truly hear and understand. This practice strengthens bonds and fosters a deeper understanding and connection.

Maintaining these connections over time requires effort and dedication. With life constantly shifting, relationships can slip away if not nurtured. Regular check-ins and updates are simple yet effective ways to stay connected. A short call, a heartfelt message, or a casual coffee date can bridge the emotional distance that time and responsibilities create. They show that you care and you are invested in maintaining the relationship. Marking milestones—whether birthdays, anniversaries, or personal victories—strengthens bonds and creates cherished memories. These shared moments create memories and a sense of belonging, reminding each other of the value you bring to one another's lives. **It's about being present, even when life pulls you in different directions, and ensuring the connection remains strong.**

Conflict is inevitable, but how you navigate it determines the strength of your bond. **Resolving conflicts constructively is crucial to maintaining harmony.** One effective technique is using 'I' statements, which express feelings without blame, preventing defensiveness and easing tension. For example, saying, "I feel upset when plans change at the last minute," is more constructive than "You always change plans." This approach opens the door to dialogue rather than defensiveness. **Active listening**—truly hearing the other person without interruption—creates space for understanding and resolution. In more complex issues, mediation strategies might be necessary. A neutral third party can facilitate communication and help reach a resolution respecting everyone's needs. Handling conflicts with care not only resolves issues but fortifies relationships, proving they can endure life's inevitable challenges.

Nurturing relationships with intentionality means making a conscious effort to deepen your connections. It's about being mindful of the relationship's needs and taking deliberate steps to meet them. Show appreciation and gratitude regularly, letting people know how much they mean to you. Small gestures, like a handwritten note or a thoughtful gift, can speak volumes. Be proactive in supporting each other through life's ups and downs, offering help or a listening ear when needed. Intentionality also involves setting aside time for meaningful interactions, whether it's a weekly catch-up or a planned activity together. These moments create space for growth and understanding, allowing relationships to flourish. Being intentional means prioritizing the relationship, even amidst life's demands, and committing to its ongoing nurturing.

5.3 CREATING A TRIBE OF SUPPORT

The concept of a "tribe" may evoke images of ancient communities gathered around a fire, sharing stories and warmth. Today, your tribe is the circle that lifts you up—a space of unwavering support, understanding, and belonging. A supportive tribe possesses characteristics that make it a powerful force in your life. It is a group marked by mutual respect, shared values, and a commitment to each other's growth. Within this circle, you find emotional refuge and practical support, allowing you to tackle life's challenges confidently. **The bonds within a tribe are not merely social; they are deeply impactful, providing a sense of belonging and identity.** This emotional bond can boost morale and give the strength to persevere through difficult times.

The first step in creating your tribe is seeking out those who share your values—people who inspire, challenge, and support you. One effective strategy is to attend interest-based meetups. These gatherings are designed to bring together people with similar passions, whether it's a love for hiking, art, or technology. By participating in these events, you naturally connect with individuals who share your interests, opening the door to meaningful relationships. Online communities—whether Facebook groups, Reddit forums, or specialized networks—offer a way to connect with like-minded individuals across the globe. The digital world offers a vast array of platforms where you can join discussions and share experiences with people across the globe. **These virtual spaces break down geographical barriers, allowing you to connect with others with similar values and aspirations.** By actively seeking out these communities, you lay the foundation for a tribe that reflects who you are and where you wish to go.

Building trust within your tribe is vital for fostering a supportive and cohesive group. **Trust is cultivated through shared experiences and the willingness to be vulnerable.** When you share your struggles, dreams, and fears, you invite others to do the same, creating mutual understanding. This openness strengthens the bonds within the tribe, as members feel more connected and invested in each other's well-being. Establishing group norms and expectations also plays a crucial role in building trust.

These guidelines ensure everyone knows what to expect and how to contribute positively to the group dynamic. By clarifying these norms, you create an environment where every member feels respected and valued, enhancing community and trust.

To solidify the bonds within your tribe, consider organizing activities that foster connection and camaraderie. These activities can range from simple gatherings to more structured events, each providing an opportunity to strengthen the community. Social outings, like a group hike or a dinner, allow for relaxed interactions where members can engage personally. Workshops or collaborative projects offer a chance to work together towards a common goal, reinforcing teamwork and shared purpose. These activities deepen relationships and create shared memories that further cement the group's unity. **By investing time and effort into these bonding experiences, you nurture a tribe that is resilient, supportive, and deeply connected.**

5.4 NETWORKING WITH INTENTION AND PURPOSE

Networking is often seen as a professional necessity but extends far beyond exchanging business cards. It is a dynamic process that is crucial for personal and professional growth. Networking unlocks resources, insights, and opportunities you may never have encountered otherwise. Whether you're seeking a career change, exploring new industries, or simply looking to learn from others, networking provides the platform to do so. **It's about creating relationships that support your journey, offering guidance, insight, and inspiration.**

To maximize the impact of networking, start by setting clear goals. Identify key individuals or organizations that align with your aspirations. Ask yourself: Who do I want to connect with, and why? Perhaps you're interested in a particular industry leader whose work you admire, or maybe there's a company whose mission resonates with your values. Determine what you hope to achieve from these connections. Are you looking for mentorship, collaboration, or exchange of ideas? By clarifying your objectives, you can approach networking with purpose and direction. This focus enhances your interactions and ensures that your efforts align with your broader goals.

Building authentic connections requires more than just surface-level interactions. **It's about creating genuine, meaningful relationships rooted in mutual interests and value exchange.** Focus on **what you can offer and what you hope to gain**. This reciprocity fosters a sense of trust and respect, laying the groundwork for lasting relationships. When meeting someone new, approach the conversation with curiosity and openness. Ask about their experiences, challenges, and achievements. Share your own stories and insights, creating an engaging and informative dialogue. Connecting personally with mentors builds rapport and establishes a foundation for future collaboration.

Networking takes place in various contexts, each offering unique opportunities to connect. You can engage with peers and leaders in your field in professional settings, such as conferences or industry events. These environments have potential for learning and growth as you exchange ideas and explore new perspectives. Social gatherings, on the other hand, offer a more relaxed atmosphere where connections can form naturally. Whether attending a dinner party or a community event, these interactions often lead to unexpected opportunities. Online platforms break geographical barriers, allowing you to network with a global audience in once-impossible ways. **You can cultivate an expansive and supportive network by leveraging these diverse environments.**

Interactive Element: Networking Goal Worksheet

Create a worksheet to guide your networking efforts. List key individuals or organizations you wish to connect with and the reasons for each. Define your desired outcomes, such as gaining insights, forming partnerships, or expanding your knowledge. Use this worksheet to prepare for networking events, ensuring that your interactions are focused and intentional. This exercise clarifies your networking goals and enhances your ability to build meaningful connections that align with your aspirations.

Networking is a powerful tool that can transform your personal and professional life when approached with intention and purpose. **By setting clear objectives, building authentic relationships, and navigating** various networking contexts, you unlock a world of possibilities that support your growth and success.

5.5 MUTUAL GROWTH THROUGH COMMUNITY BUILDING

Post-event interactions provide a valuable chance to discover new resources and opportunities. We can discover varied expertise through social interactions that may result in collaborations. Attending an event catered to a common interest also benefits each participant. **This interaction is the essence of mutual growth within a community**—a dynamic environment where personal development is intertwined with collective progress. In such spaces, shared learning experiences become the norm. When individuals come together with the intent to learn, they create an atmosphere of growth. Think of peer-led workshops or seminars where each member contributes their expertise, leading sessions that enlighten others while honing their skills. This knowledge exchange turns the community into a living library, with each person as a teacher and a student.

Communities thrive on systems of accountability, where members encourage each other to set and reach personal goals. Picture a group of writers meeting weekly to share their progress. They hold each other accountable, providing motivation and support while navigating the challenges of creative endeavors. This collaborative accountability ensures that individual goals are pursued with the added momentum of collective encouragement. It's like a fitness class where participants push one another to keep going, knowing they're not alone in their efforts. This way, **accountability becomes a shared responsibility, driving personal and collective achievements.**

Creating growth-oriented activities within a community fosters an environment of continuous development. Book clubs or study groups can be particularly effective, encouraging members to explore new ideas and perspectives. Consider a book club that explores different themes monthly—historical fiction one month, contemporary issues the next—fostering insightful discussions and diverse perspectives. Diverse topics expand perspectives, challenge existing beliefs, and encourage meaningful discussions. Through both the readings and shared conversations, members gain valuable insights that deepen their understanding of the world and their role within it. These gatherings serve as a ground for fresh ideas, leaving participants inspired and empowered with new knowledge and experience they gained.

Skill-sharing is one of the most impactful mechanisms in community building, fostering a culture where knowledge and expertise flow freely between members. When members share their skills and knowledge, everyone benefits. Skill-swap events, such as weekend workshops or exchange meetups, provide a platform where individuals can teach their expertise, like photography or coding, while simultaneously learning from others. For instance, a community might organize a weekend workshop where one person teaches photography basics while another offers a crash course in coding. The result is a vibrant exchange where skills are taught and applied, leading to a deeper understanding and proficiency. Collaborative teaching sessions—where members co-create workshops or joint projects—further enhance this dynamic, enabling individuals to apply their collective skills in real-world scenarios. **This collaboration strengthens individual capabilities and builds a sense of unity and shared purpose.**

A culture of feedback and continuous improvement is the backbone of any thriving community, fostering both growth and emotional resilience. Constructive feedback fuels continuous learning, with each member offering insights and suggestions that help others sharpen their skills and expand their knowledge. Consider a group of amateur chefs who meet to cook and critique each other's dishes. They provide feedback on flavor, presentation, and technique, helping each member improve their culinary prowess. This open exchange fosters an environment where continuous improvement is not only welcomed but actively encouraged, benefiting the entire community by lifting everyone's abilities. It creates a safe space for experimentation, where mistakes are viewed as opportunities for learning rather than failures. **By embracing feedback, the community cultivates a collective growth mindset, where every member supports one another's journey toward personal and collective improvement.**

Communities that prioritize mutual growth create fertile ground for personal and collective development. Through shared learning experiences, structured accountability systems, and skill-sharing initiatives, such as collaborative workshops, members enhance their abilities while advancing the community's collective progress. Such communities become more than just a collection of individuals; **they evolve into ecosystems where growth is nurtured and potential is realized.**

5.6 LEVERAGING SUPPORT NETWORKS FOR RESILIENCE

When you think about resilience, you might picture a lone figure braving the storm. Yet, true resilience isn't solitary; it often thrives through connection with others. **Community contexts create an environment where resilience is nurtured through collective strength and support.** These networks serve as emotional buffers, offering the encouragement and empathy needed to weather life's challenges—from everyday stress to more serious hardships. Imagine being part of a group where every member brings their presence, experiences, and insights. This shared space becomes a sanctuary, where resilience is nurtured not just individually, but as a collective force, strengthened by the bonds between us.

In challenging times, tapping into community resources can be a lifeline. Local support groups, mental health organizations, or hobby clubs provide a range of services and activities that help you navigate stress. Whether it's a group focused on mental wellness, a fitness club, or a professional mentorship program, these resources create platforms for connection, growth, and shared learning. They offer a safe space to share struggles, gain new perspectives, and find solutions. Accessing these resources encourages you to step out of isolation and into a network that reinforces your resilience. **The knowledge that others face similar challenges can be a powerful motivator, reminding you that you're not alone in your journey.**

Building a resilient community mindset requires cultivating adaptability and growth. It begins with sharing success stories and lessons learned—creating a collective wisdom that strengthens the entire group. It starts with sharing success stories and lessons learned, creating a cumulation of wisdom from which the entire community benefits. These stories of triumph and perseverance inspire hope, showing us that setbacks aren't dead ends—they're stepping stones toward growth. By exchanging these stories, members learn from each other's experiences, gaining insights that help them tackle their challenges with renewed strength. **This shared learning fosters a culture of resilience, where adaptability becomes second nature, and the community thrives in the face of adversity.**

Preparing for future challenges requires foresight and collaboration. Regular meetings to discuss potential risks and devise contingency plans can turn uncertainty into readiness. These sessions foster open dialogue and collective problem-solving, allowing members to contribute their skills and ideas to ensure the community's preparedness. By anticipating challenges and proactively planning responses, the community becomes a cohesive unit, ready to face whatever comes its way. **This collective preparedness strengthens individual resilience and enhances the community's ability to adapt and evolve in an ever-changing world.** It creates a strong foundation where each member feels supported, knowing the group is equipped to weather any storm.

As we wrap up this chapter on building supportive communities, it's clear how essential these networks are in fostering resilience. They offer both emotional support and practical resources, empowering us to face life's challenges with confidence. In the next chapter, we'll explore how emotional intelligence plays a key role in strengthening these connections and enhancing personal resilience.

A Circle of Strength

I walked alone, my voice so still,
A heart that ached, a void to fill.
In silence, longing for a hand,
A place where I could understand.
But now I know, I'm not alone,
A world of voices like my own.

The power thrives in bonds we weave,
A net of strength when hearts believe.
Through love and trust, we heal the scars,
Each soul a beacon, shining stars.
From family's touch to friendships true,
Our roots grow deep, our skies turn blue.

To build these ties, we step with grace,
We meet, we share, we find our place.
Through words exchanged and hearts laid bare,
Connections bloom with love and care.
A simple smile, a kind hello,
A bridge where lonely rivers flow.

Within our tribes, we find our might,
Where trust and warmth ignite the night.
Shared goals, shared dreams, a common thread,
With open arms, we move ahead.
Together strong, we lift, we rise,
A family formed beyond the ties.

Networking grows with heart and mind,
In circles rich with dreams aligned.
We reach beyond, we cast our net,
With purpose clear, our goals are set.
In every voice, in every space,
We find our strength, we find our place.

Resilience thrives when we unite,
A shield against life's fiercest fight.
With hands entwined and spirits bold,
We face the storms, we brave the cold.
Through every step, through highs and lows,
Our strength in unity still grows.

6

INTEGRATING MINDFULNESS AND SELF-CARE

"Amidst the rush of my duties, I found peace in fleeting moments when I could admire the world from above. The sunrises and sunsets captivated me, their colors dancing on the water. On quiet night flights, as passengers slept, I would rest in my seat and gaze out the window, letting the soft moonlight soothe me. It was a brief but welcome escape from the busyness of my responsibilities."

6.1 THE ROLE OF MINDFULNESS IN RESILIENCE

Picture a bustling city street. The traffic noise and passersby's hurried pace create a symphony of chaos. Amidst this, a single tree stands, its leaves rustling gently in the breeze, a beacon of calm in a sea of activity. Mindfulness is much like that tree. It is the practice of anchoring oneself in the present moment, observing thoughts and feelings without judgment. Rooted in ancient Eastern traditions, this time-honored practice offers a sense of calm and clarity in today's often chaotic world. Over time, mindfulness has seamlessly integrated into modern psychology and wellness, providing practical tools to improve mental well-being and build resilience.

Mindfulness is an abstract concept and a powerful tool for building resilience. You can reduce stress and maintain emotional balance, even in challenging circumstances, by cultivating awareness. Research has shown that mindfulness can lower cortisol levels, a hormone associated with stress, helping you manage difficult emotions more effectively. Individuals who regularly practice mindfulness report greater resilience, as they are less likely to be overwhelmed by negative thoughts and feelings. Instead, **mindfulness allows them to observe these emotions from a distance, disrupting the cycle of negative thought patterns and preventing emotional shutdowns.** This practice fosters a sense of self-compassion, promoting higher levels of happiness and life satisfaction.

Mindfulness-Based Stress Reduction (MBSR), developed by Jon Kabat-Zinn, is a structured program designed to reduce stress and improve emotional health. It combines mindfulness meditation, body awareness, and yoga for a holistic approach to well-being. Participants often experience improvements in anxiety, depression, and self-compassion. Key components of the program include guided meditation to cultivate present-moment awareness, cognitive restructuring to reframe negative thoughts, and exercises that integrate mindfulness into daily life. MBSR helps participants feel more centered and resilient, better equipped to navigate life's challenges.

Incorporating mindfulness into daily life doesn't require extensive time or resources. Simple practices can have a profound impact on your well-being. Start by focusing on everyday activities. For example, as you sip your morning coffee, tune into the aroma, the warmth of the mug, and the taste of each sip. On a walk, pay attention to the sensation of your feet on the ground and the rhythm of your breath. These moments help center your attention in the present, bringing clarity and reducing stress. Mindfulness is simpler to integrate into your life than you might think, and it's incredibly effective.

Mindfulness can also be practiced through brief **meditation sessions.** For instance, you can find a quiet space, sit comfortably, and focus on your breath for 5-10 minutes. Notice the rise and fall of your chest and the air entering and leaving your body. If your mind wanders, gently guide your focus back to your breath. This practice, even for a few minutes daily, can significantly reduce stress and enhance emotional resilience.

Reflection Section: Mindfulness in Action

As you explore mindfulness, take a moment each day to reflect on your practice. Consider keeping a journal where you note your experiences and any changes in your stress levels or emotional balance. Reflect on how mindfulness has impacted your daily life—what moments felt especially grounding or calming? What challenges did you encounter? Journaling these insights can deepen your practice and offer valuable insights into your personal growth and resilience.

Have you ever paused to truly experience the present moment? Embracing mindfulness is an ongoing practice that shifts how you engage with the world, helping you find meaning in each moment. **Through mindfulness, you cultivate a sense of presence, balance, and strength,**

equipping yourself to face challenges with resilience and grace. As you integrate these practices into your life, you discover the profound impact of mindfulness on your overall well-being, transforming how you experience the world and navigate its complexities.

6.2 SELF-CARE PRACTICES FOR EMOTIONAL HEALTH

Self-care is a term that has gained popularity, but its essence can sometimes be misunderstood. At its core, self-care is the intentional act of nurturing your physical, emotional, and mental well-being. **It focuses on maintaining balance and nurturing your well-being.** However, self-care differs from indulgence; while indulgence offers temporary pleasure, true self-care fosters long-term well-being. **Proper self-care is more about creating a lifestyle supporting physical, emotional, social, and spiritual health.** It involves making choices that replenish your energy and keep you grounded. Focusing on genuine self-care fosters resilience and emotional stability, equipping yourself to face life's challenges with a **clear mind and a light heart.**

To make self-care truly effective, start by identifying your personal needs—what fuels you, what drains you, and what restores your balance. Each person's self-care requirements are unique, shaped by their lifestyle, preferences, and personal challenges. Assessing your self-care needs begins with **introspection and reflection.** Consider using self-care assessment tools to better understand your current practices and areas that need attention. These tools often cover various aspects of well-being, prompting you to think about your physical health, emotional state, and social interactions. **Reflective exercises** can also help you pinpoint what indeed recharges you. Ask yourself, "What activities make me feel most relaxed?" or "What do I need to feel emotionally fulfilled?" Understanding your needs allows you to tailor a self-care plan that genuinely supports you, acknowledging that self-care is not one-size-fits-all but adaptable to your unique needs.

Creating a self-care plan is similar to designing a blueprint for your well-being. It requires a thoughtful approach to balance the different aspects of your life. Start by setting realistic goals that address each area of well-being. Consider incorporating regular exercise, a balanced diet, and adequate sleep into your routine for **physical self-care. Emotional self-care** might involve setting boundaries, practicing gratitude, or engaging in creative activities that bring joy. **Socially,** nurturing supportive relationships and connecting with loved ones can enhance your sense of belonging. **Spiritually,** you might explore practices that align with your beliefs, such as meditation, prayer, or time in nature. **By developing a comprehensive self-care plan, you create a framework that supports your overall health and happiness.**

Despite the importance of self-care, many face barriers that hinder its consistent practice. Common obstacles include time constraints, guilt, or the perception that self-care is selfish. It's essential to address these barriers head-on. **Time management is critical; prioritizing self-care in your schedule affirms its value.** Consider setting aside specific times dedicated to self-care activities each day, treating them as non-negotiable appointments with yourself. Overcoming guilt involves shifting your mindset—view self-care as an essential investment, much like charging a phone or refueling a car, rather than an indulgence. Remember, taking care of yourself is not selfish; it enables you to be more present and practical in your relationships and responsibilities. Acknowledging these barriers and working to overcome them pave the way for sustainable self-care practices.

Interactive Element: Personal Self-Care Audit

When was the last time you truly checked in with yourself? Take a moment to conduct a personal self-care audit. List areas where you currently practice self-care and note any gaps you observe. Consider using a self-care assessment tool to guide this process, reflecting on your physical, emotional, social, and spiritual well-being. Identify one or two areas where you can enhance your self-care routine. Then, commit to a small but meaningful change—something you can start today. This audit is a starting point for developing a personalized self-care plan that aligns with your unique requirements and aspirations.

6.3 MINDFULNESS MEDITATION TECHNIQUES

With the constant buzz of notifications, deadlines, and responsibilities, finding a moment of peace can feel impossible. Yet, within this chaos lies the opportunity for **mindfulness meditation**—a practice that invites you to pause, breathe, and center yourself. There are various meditation techniques, each offering unique benefits. One way to cultivate mindfulness is through **focused attention meditation**, a practice that strengthens concentration and calms the mind. It requires you to concentrate on a single object, thought, or sensation, such as your breath or a candle flame. **This focus helps quiet the mind, reducing the mental chatter that often fuels stress and anxiety.** By training your attention, you cultivate a sense of calm and clarity, enhancing your ability to remain present in any situation.

Another powerful approach is **open-monitoring meditation**, which helps you develop awareness by observing thoughts without attachment. Unlike focused attention, this technique encourages you to observe your thoughts and feelings as they arise without judgment or attachment. Imagine sitting by a river, watching the water flow by—each thought is a leaf carried gently downstream. Instead of clinging to these thoughts, you simply acknowledge them and let them pass. You notice them, but you don't cling to them. **This practice fosters a deep awareness of your mental landscape, helping you understand your habitual thought patterns and emotional responses.** Over time, open monitoring meditation cultivates a sense of acceptance and composure, allowing you to navigate life's challenges with greater ease and insight.

Guided meditation offers a structured approach to mindfulness, providing step-by-step instructions to help you relax and focus. One popular technique is the **body scan meditation**. This practice involves lying down or sitting comfortably, then slowly directing your attention to each part of your body, from your toes to the top of your head. As you focus on each area, notice any sensations, tension, or discomfort. The goal is not to change these feelings but to acknowledge them with a gentle awareness. **This meditation not only fosters relaxation but also**

increases body awareness, helping you recognize and release physical tension more effectively.

Another powerful guided meditation is **loving-kindness meditation**, which encourages compassion and empathy. Begin by finding a comfortable position and closing your eyes. Picture someone you care about, and silently repeat phrases like, "**May you be happy, may you be healthy, may you be safe.**" Gradually extend these wishes to yourself, then to others in your life, and eventually to all beings. This practice gently opens your heart, allowing you to feel warmth and connection—not just toward others, but also toward yourself. **It helps dissolve barriers of judgment and resentment, allowing compassion to flourish.**

Have you ever wondered why some people seem effortlessly calm and centered? Establishing a regular meditation habit unlocks the full benefits of mindfulness, helping you cultivate inner peace and focus. Start by setting a dedicated time each day for your practice. Whether it's five minutes in the morning or thirty minutes before bed, **consistency is more important than duration.** Designate a peaceful meditation space, free from distractions, where you can sit comfortably. Soft lighting, a calming scent, or a cozy cushion can transform this area into a personal sanctuary. Personalize your space with cushions, blankets, or a favorite chair—elements that invite relaxation. Over time, this spot will become your refuge, a retreat from the demands of daily life.

Does your mind race the moment you sit in silence? Many beginners struggle with restlessness, impatience, and doubt when starting a meditation practice. It's essential to approach these challenges with curiosity and kindness rather than self-criticism. If your mind wanders, simply return to your breath, a repeated mantra, or the gentle rhythm of ambient sounds around you. Meditation **is not about achieving a blank mind but developing awareness.** Over time, these challenges often diminish as your practice deepens. For extra support, try joining a meditation group or using guided apps—these can provide structure, motivation, and a sense of community, making your practice easier to sustain. These resources can provide structure, guidance, and a sense of community, making staying committed to your routine more manageable.

6.4 JOURNALING FOR SELF-REFLECTION AND GROWTH

Imagine the quiet rustle of paper, the smooth glide of your pen—before you lies a blank page, ready to capture your thoughts as they flow freely. **Journaling is a practice that offers a window into your inner world, helping to clarify the thoughts and emotions that often swirl in your mind.** It is a powerful tool for personal development, allowing you to articulate feelings that might otherwise remain unexamined. You untangle complex emotions through writing, gaining insight into your reactions and behaviors. This practice nurtures self-awareness, offering a judgment-free space to explore your ideas, emotions, and aspirations. **As you write, you engage in a dialogue with yourself, uncovering hidden fears and desires and discovering new pathways to growth.**

Different journaling techniques cater to varied needs, each offering unique benefits. Ever tried writing without stopping to think? **Stream-of-consciousness journaling** lets you capture thoughts exactly as they arise—raw, unfiltered, and revealing. This approach lets you tap into your subconscious, revealing patterns and insights that might elude conscious reflection. It is a liberating practice, one that encourages authenticity and spontaneity.

On the other hand, **gratitude journaling** focuses on recognizing and appreciating the positive aspects of life. By regularly noting things you are grateful for, you cultivate a mindset of abundance and positivity. **This practice shifts your focus from what is lacking to what is present, fostering contentment and resilience.**

Prompt-based journaling provides structure and deeper insight. Questions like "What are my core values?" or "What challenges have shaped me?" guide you toward meaningful self-discovery. Consider prompts that encourage introspection, such as "What are my core values?" or "How have I grown in the past year?" These questions prompt you to reflect deeply, examining your beliefs and experiences. Another powerful prompt might be, "What challenges have I overcome, and what have they taught me?" By engaging with these questions, you gain clarity and perspective, understanding how past experiences have shaped who you are today. **This practice enhances**

self-awareness and empowers you to set intentions for future growth.

Journals serve as valuable tools for goal setting and tracking progress. By documenting your aspirations and outlining steps to achieve them, you create a roadmap for success. Begin by identifying specific goals, whether personal, professional, or creative. Break these goals into actionable steps, and use your journal to monitor your progress. Regularly reviewing your entries provides motivation and accountability, reminding you of your commitments and achievements. It also offers an opportunity to adjust goals, ensuring they remain relevant and aligned with your aspirations. **This process transforms your journal into a dynamic tool for personal development that supports realizing your potential.**

Reflection Section: Journaling Prompts for Growth

Consider incorporating regular reflection into your journaling practice. Use prompts such as "What are my strengths, and how can I use them more effectively?" or "What fears are holding me back, and how can I overcome them?" Reflect on these questions in your journal, exploring the insights they reveal. This exercise enhances self-awareness and encourages proactive steps toward personal growth. As you engage with these prompts, you deepen your understanding of yourself, fostering a greater sense of empowerment and purpose.

Journaling is more than just writing; it is a transformative practice that nurtures self-reflection and growth. By exploring different techniques and engaging with prompts, you unlock the potential within yourself, paving the way for a more fulfilled and intentional life. You create a space for introspection and discovery through journaling, charting a course toward a future that aligns with your true self.

6.5 BALANCING MIND AND BODY WELLNESS

Think of your body and mind as two sides of the same coin—when one thrives, the other follows. Just as physical exhaustion can cloud your thoughts, mental stress can manifest in the body. This interconnectedness means that taking care of your physical health can profoundly affect your mental well-being. Physical activity strengthens your body, lifts your mood, and eases anxiety by triggering endorphin release—the brain's natural feel-good chemicals. When you exercise regularly, your brain releases endorphins, often called "feel-good" hormones. These natural mood lifters can lead to a more positive outlook on life. Exercise also reduces levels of stress hormones, such as adrenaline and cortisol, leading to a sense of calm and relaxation. **You create a harmonious balance supporting physical and mental health by nurturing your body.**

Incorporating **physical activities** into your routine is a form of self-care that pays dividends in energy and happiness. There are many exercises to explore, each offering unique benefits. **Yoga** seamlessly blends movement, breath, and stillness. With each stretch and inhale, you enhance flexibility while cultivating mental clarity. It's a practice that connects the mind and body, fostering peace and mindfulness. **Tai chi,** often described as "meditation in motion," involves slow, graceful movements and deep breathing, enhancing balance and reducing stress. With its rhythmic and high-energy routines, **Aerobics** boosts cardiovascular health and releases pent-up energy, leaving you invigorated and refreshed. By choosing activities that resonate with you, you ensure that exercise becomes an enjoyable and sustainable part of your life.

Mindful eating strengthens the mind-body connection. Imagine savoring each bite—appreciating its texture, aroma, and flavor—rather than rushing through a meal distractedly. It involves being fully present during meals, savoring each bite, and listening to your body's hunger and fullness cues. This approach encourages you to slow down and appreciate your food's flavors, textures, and aromas, turning every meal into a rich sensory experience. Mindful eating can help prevent overeating and promote a healthier relationship with food. It invites you to recognize when you're truly hungry versus eating out of habit or emotional need. By fostering a deeper awareness of your eating habits, you make more conscious and nourishing choices that benefit your overall health.

Creating a balanced lifestyle means integrating practices supporting your mental and physical well-being. Start by establishing a routine with regular physical activity, as consistency is key to experiencing its full benefits, from improved mood to increased energy. Incorporate mindful eating into your meals, focusing on the quality rather than the quantity of food. Balancing work and leisure by setting boundaries and prioritizing downtime allows you to recharge and maintain your mental health. Consider exploring hobbies that engage both body and mind, such as **gardening, dancing, or hiking**. These activities not only provide physical benefits but also offer **mental and emotional enrichment.**

As you cultivate a lifestyle that nurtures both body and mind, you lay the foundation for a truly holistic approach to wellness. **This balance fosters resilience, equipping you to handle stress and challenges with poise and strength.** By embracing practices that nurture every aspect of your being, you create a foundation for a fulfilling and vibrant life.

6.6 SUSTAINING WELL-BEING THROUGH DAILY RITUALS

Amid the constant changes of daily life, rituals serve as reliable anchors, bringing a sense of stability and reassurance. Unlike rigid routines, **rituals are carried out with intention and purpose, offering moments of grounding and connection.** They provide comfort and continuity, helping us navigate life's uncertainties calmly and consistently. Engaging in daily rituals helps sustain emotional and physical health by creating moments of stillness and reflection. They allow us to pause, breathe, and connect with ourselves, fostering a sense of well-being that permeates every aspect of our lives. We cultivate habits that nurture our bodies and minds by embedding these practices into our daily rhythm, supporting a balanced and fulfilling existence.

Designing personal rituals is an opportunity to craft moments that resonate deeply with your values and aspirations. Morning rituals, for instance, set the tone for the day ahead. Consider beginning your day with quiet reflection and a warm cup of tea or coffee. This simple act can become a sacred time to contemplate your intentions and goals, creating a sense of purpose and direction. Alternatively, you might engage in gentle stretching or yoga, awakening your body and mind with mindful movement.

On the other hand, evening rituals offer a chance to unwind and release the day's tensions. A warm bath, accompanied by soothing music or a favorite book, can provide a gentle transition into rest. **By incorporating these rituals into your daily routine, you create a framework that supports your overall well-being, nourishing your spirit and enhancing your resilience.**

Nature's inherent tranquility and beauty can be a powerful element in daily rituals. Integrating nature into your practices invites a sense of peace and connection to the world around you. Consider taking a daily walk in a nearby park or garden, allowing the sights and sounds of nature to envelop your senses. As you stroll, notice the rustle of leaves, birds chirping, and the sun's warmth on your skin. These moments of immersion in nature can provide a respite from the demands of modern life, offering a space to recharge and reflect. If walking isn't feasible, consider bringing elements of nature into your home—a potted plant, a vase of fresh flowers, or a small water fountain can evoke a sense of calm and serenity. **By weaving nature into your rituals, you cultivate an environment that nurtures both body and soul, enhancing your capacity for resilience and well-being.**

As life evolves, so too should your rituals. Evaluating and adjusting these practices ensures they continue to serve your needs and support your well-being. Periodically assess your rituals, reflecting on their impact and relevance to your current circumstances. Are they providing the intended benefits, or do they feel more like obligations? If a ritual no longer resonates, consider modifying it or introducing a new practice that aligns with your present needs and goals. This flexibility allows your rituals to grow with you, adapting to changes in your life while maintaining their core purpose. **By regularly revisiting and refining your rituals, you ensure they remain meaningful and effective, enhancing their ability to sustain your well-being.**

In closing this chapter, we've explored the power of daily rituals to nurture both mind and body. These practices become enduring sources of strength and balance when thoughtfully designed and regularly evaluated. As we move forward, we'll delve into the next chapter, exploring how to cultivate community and connection, further enriching our journey toward a more harmonious and resilient life.

The Strength Within:

Amid the chaos, life unfolds,
A constant rush, a tale retold.
Yet mindfulness, a steady guide,
Brings peace within, lets fears subside.
Through gentle breaths and present sights,
We find our calm in fleeting nights.

Resilience blooms when stress runs high,
With mindful thoughts, we touch the sky.
Observe the mind, let worries drift,
In quiet moments lies our gift.
With every breath, we learn to cope,
Releasing fear, embracing hope.

Self-care, a path both wise and kind,
A balance sought in heart and mind.
It's not indulgence, but a way,
To fuel our strength for each new day.
By knowing needs and tending well,
We build a life where we excel.

Through mindful acts, we find our space,
A simple walk, a slowing pace.
From morning light to evening's close,
In daily rituals, strength still grows.
Each moment savored, thought embraced,
Becomes a step, a life retraced.

The mind and body, hand in hand,
In motion thrive, together stand.
A gentle stretch, a mindful meal,
A steady pulse, a way to heal.
By honoring both, we start to see,
The harmony that sets us free.

Through reflection, growth takes form,
Like seeds that thrive through sun and storm.
With journals filled and goals aligned,
We shape our path, our dreams defined.
In every word, a truth is found,
A journey built on solid ground.

7

HARNESSING REAL-LIFE NARRATIVES

> "A severe storm was predicted to hit the city, forcing aircraft to be relocated for safety. Amid this scary problem, I was among the crew assigned to man one of these aircraft alongside the rest of the cabin team. The prospect of flying in the face of such scary, bad weather filled me with dread. Without passengers on board, I questioned the necessity of our presence in the cabin. "It's for safety," according to the management, yet doubts scared me. Whose safety were we ensuring? I wondered about our safety while protecting the aircraft from the storm's danger. The fear of flying, especially under such precarious conditions, sat in. I contemplated voicing my concerns about feeling airsick to the captain, but my youthful, inexperienced, and confused mind held me back. The captain in charge of the flight had a duty to fulfill: to secure the aircraft's safety. And we, the cabin crew on board, have our responsibilities, too. We needed to be on board to support the cockpit crew in completing the mission."

Imagine standing at the helm of a ship, the horizon vast and unknown, the sea unpredictable and fierce. This is the essence of leadership in its rawest form—a journey where vision, empathy, and decisiveness guide the vessel through uncharted waters. Resilient leaders stand firm against the storm, eyes locked on the horizon, steering with unwavering resolve. They possess a unique blend of traits that enable them to overcome challenges for themselves and those they lead. Vision allows them to see beyond the immediate turmoil, envisioning a future that inspires and motivates. Empathy connects them to their crew, understanding their fears and aspirations and fostering a sense of unity and shared purpose. Decisiveness, that unwavering ability to make tough calls under pressure, ensures progress even when the path is unclear. These leaders are not born but built, shaped by the crises they face and the resilience they cultivate within themselves.

7.1 LEARNING FROM INSPIRATIONAL LEADERS

Throughout history, leaders have inspired us through their dedication and devotion to their sworn duties. Anwar Ibrahim, the Prime Minister of Malaysia, is a striking example of resilience in leadership. Despite enduring significant hardship, including imprisonment, he emerged victorious and continues to mobilize positive change Anwar's political journey has been marked by resilience and perseverance. In the late 1990s, while serving as Deputy Prime Minister, he was dismissed and subsequently imprisoned on charges widely viewed as politically motivated. After his release, he became a key figure in Malaysia's opposition, leading his coalition to unprecedented electoral victories. Despite facing additional legal challenges and imprisonment, Anwar remained a steadfast advocate for reform. His appointment in November 2022, after more than two decades of political struggle, marked a historic victory over adversity and a turning point for Malaysia. As Prime Minister, he has prioritized anti-corruption efforts, economic reform, and the strengthening of democratic institutions, striving to unify and advance Malaysia. **His authenticity, grounded in steadfast core values, inspired a nation to rise above hatred and division.**

Ibrahim's leadership was not just about overcoming adversity but transforming it into a force for change. This proves that true leadership is inseparable from resilience and the compassion needed to heal a nation. The transformative power of resilience in leadership reminds us that challenges are opportunities for growth and change.

In the modern era, we witness CEOs navigating economic downturns with similar resilience and ingenuity. These leaders face the challenge of maintaining stability in volatile markets, requiring a delicate balance of vision and realism. During crises, they demonstrate self-sacrifice, earning trust and commitment from their teams. During the 2008 financial crisis, leaders like Howard Schultz (Starbucks) and Alan Mulally (Ford) made bold decisions to stabilize their companies. Some took pay cuts or restructured operations to ensure their employees' livelihoods. Their ability to communicate transparently about these actions while providing direction and support fostered a sense of solidarity and shared purpose. **Such leadership is not about wielding power but empowering others, creating an environment where everyone feels valued and invested in the collective success.**

These stories of leadership offer valuable lessons for personal development. **The traits that enable leaders to thrive in adversity—vision, empathy, and decisiveness—can be cultivated in our lives. Vision** is about setting clear goals and maintaining focus, even when distractions abound. **Empathy** involves actively listening to others, understanding their perspectives, and building connections that strengthen relationships. **Decisiveness** requires the courage to make choices, learn from successes and mistakes, and adapt. **By embodying these qualities, we can navigate our challenges with resilience and purpose, becoming leaders in our own right, whether in our families, communities, or workplaces.**

Reflection Section: Leadership Traits Self-Assessment

Consider the traits of vision, empathy, and decisiveness. Reflect on a recent challenge you faced and how you exhibited these qualities. What did this experience teach you about your leadership strengths? Where do you see room for growth? Write down specific actions—such as improving communication, practicing active listening, or making bold decisions—that can strengthen your leadership in both personal and professional settings. This exercise encourages self-awareness and growth, helping you develop the resilience and leadership skills needed to thrive in adversity. It's a journey of self-discovery and commitment, a path toward becoming the best version of yourself.

Exploring these leadership narratives reveals **that resilience is not a solitary endeavor but a collective journey. It is about lifting others as we rise, creating a legacy of strength and compassion that endures beyond our trials.**

7.2 OVERCOMING ADVERSITY: PERSONAL SUCCESS STORIES

Imagine waking up each day with a determination that defies the odds stacked against you. This scenario is the reality for many individuals who have triumphed over physical disabilities. Take, for example, Nicholas James Vujicic, born without arms and legs due to amelia-tetra syndrome. Rather than allowing his condition to define him, he embraced his uniqueness and transformed his life. He turned his struggles into a message of hope, becoming a world-renowned motivational speaker who teaches self-acceptance and perseverance. **His story is not just about overcoming a physical limitation; it's a testament to the resilience of the human spirit.** Through sheer will and an unwavering belief in his potential, he turned what many would consider an insurmountable obstacle into a platform for empowerment and change. **His journey underscores the power of resilience, showing that physical limitations do not dictate one's capacity for success.**

Few stories illustrate financial resilience better than that of Milton S. Hershey, who overcame failure to build an empire. Milton S. Hershey, the founder of the Hershey Chocolate Company, experienced significant financial setbacks before achieving success. In 1882, after six years of running a candy store in Philadelphia, Hershey faced bankruptcy due to the store's failure. Undeterred, he returned to Lancaster, Pennsylvania, where he founded the Lancaster Caramel Company—a breakthrough success that paved the way for his chocolate empire. He later sold this company for $1 million in 1900 to focus on perfecting milk chocolate production, leading to the creation of the Hershey Chocolate Company. This venture evolved into a thriving enterprise, making the Hershey family name synonymous with chocolate. Milton Hershey's journey from bankruptcy to building a successful business empire exemplifies resilience and determination in the face of financial adversity. With persistence, Milton Hershey recovered financially and thrived, creating a legacy for their children. This narrative highlights the importance of adaptability in the face of adversity. It reminds us that setbacks, while daunting, are often the precursors to growth and reinvention. By embracing change and learning from failure, they transformed a dire situation into a story of triumph and renewal.

Common threads weave through these stories, painting a picture of what it takes to overcome adversity. **Persistence** stands out as a recurring theme—a relentless drive that keeps individuals moving forward, no matter how daunting the obstacles. **It's the refusal to give up, even when the path seems impossible. Adaptability** and the ability to pivot and adjust to new circumstances with creativity and courage are also crucial.

Together, these qualities—bolstered by community support—create an unshakable foundation for success. The embrace of a supportive network—whether family, friends, or mentors—provides a safety net, offering encouragement and resources that bolster resilience. These elements are traits and lifelines guiding individuals through the storm.

Personal narratives are as diverse as they are compelling. A family friend was widowed as a young wife, left with four children to take care of. As a single parent and dedicated teacher, she worked tirelessly to provide for her children. Her children are now thriving in their fields. Two are doctors; one is an engineer and a successful financial consultant. Balancing work and family, she pursued education and professional development, driven by the desire to create a better life for her children. Her professional and profound personal success is a testament to her tenacity and love.

Similarly, immigrants often face cultural and linguistic barriers when settling in unfamiliar lands. Yet, many not only adapt but thrive. Their resilience and hard work have led them to excel, making invaluable contributions to their communities. **Their journeys are woven with courage and resilience, navigating unfamiliar landscapes with open hearts and unwavering determination.** These accounts broaden our understanding of success, revealing it as multifaceted and deeply personal.

Practical insights emerge from these stories, offering guidance for anyone facing challenges.

> **First, cultivate persistence.** Success is rarely a straight path—it often demands repeated efforts and relentless dedication.
> **Second, cultivate adaptability.** Be willing to change course, innovate, and learn from setbacks.
> **Lastly, build and cherish a strong support system.** Whether through family, friends, or mentors, surrounding yourself with uplifting individuals provides strength in times of need.

These stories remind us that adversity, while challenging, is an opportunity for growth. They inspire us to look beyond our circumstances,

see potential where others see obstacles, and write our stories of triumph.

Real-Life Case Studies in Courage

Envision receiving an urgent late-night phone call, with children's cries audible in the background, as a voice informs you of a loved one's struggle with substance abuse. The room's darkness reflects the gravity of the decision you now face, standing at a crossroads where courage must overcome the fear of the unknown. **Courage in this context is not just about being brave. It's about stepping into a situation fraught with emotional turmoil and ambiguity.** It involves taking action to rescue a family member, not knowing the outcome, yet driven by love and the hope of recovery. **This involvement is courage in its rawest form—choosing to stand by someone when the path is riddled with uncertainty.**

As decisions unfold, ethical dilemmas surface, testing the boundaries of **personal sacrifice.** Consider the mental strain of caring for a family member with **mental illness**, where your emotional well-being hangs in the balance. The courageous decision to seek help, whether through therapy or community support, reflects an understanding of one's limits. It acknowledges that courage sometimes means recognizing when you need assistance rather than shouldering the burden alone. This decision-making process involves weighing the risks to your mental state against the potential benefits of providing care. **It's a delicate dance of empathy and self-preservation, requiring a deep well of inner strength to navigate the complexities of love and responsibility.**

Courage manifests in varied and unexpected ways across different fields. Scientific discovery often involves **challenging established norms and venturing into the unknown.** Scientists who push the boundaries of knowledge demonstrate courage by pursuing ideas that defy conventional wisdom, risking failure and criticism in seeking truth. **Their courage is rooted in a relentless curiosity and a commitment to innovation, driving progress that can reshape our understanding of the world.** Similarly, **artistic courage emerges when creators challenge societal norms through their work.** Artists who use their medium to address controversial issues or tell stories often silenced display a boldness that inspires dialogue and change. **They risk rejection and censorship, yet they persist, driven by a desire to illuminate the human experience and provoke thought.**

These acts of courage, whether in personal life or professional pursuits, offer valuable lessons. **They teach us that courage is not the absence of fear but the decision to act despite it. It's about taking calculated risks and accepting the possibility of failure as part of the process.** Importantly, **courage often involves collaboration and seeking support.** The most courageous individuals recognize the strength in asking for help and building a community around them. They understand that courage does not require isolation but thrives in connection with others who share their vision and values.

Examining these real-world case studies reveals that courage manifests in various personal forms. It encompasses the quiet determination to confront challenges, the unwavering commitment to truth, and the boldness to question established norms. These narratives highlight the remarkable capacity within each individual to drive change and live genuinely. **In its many forms, courage encourages us to step beyond our fears and limitations, paving a path that is uniquely our own.**

7.4 TRANSFORMATIVE JOURNEYS FROM HELPLESSNESS TO HOPE

A loved one sits in a dimly lit room, haunted by memories that cling to his past. The person tries to occupy himself by drawing on the white canvas, ignoring the evil whispers. The weight of addiction bears down, a constant reminder of the battles he is fighting in silence. Yet, within this darkness, a flicker of hope emerges. That flicker comes from your heart as you watch, willing him to see the hope you hold for him. You want him to see and feel that hope because you love him immensely and **want him to heal more than he wants for himself.**

Transformation doesn't begin with grand gestures but with small, intentional steps toward change. It's the decision to attend that first meeting, to reach out for help, and to confront the inner demons that have long dictated the narrative. These stories of recovery are not just about abstaining from substances but about rediscovering the self and **rebuilding a life filled with purpose and connection. For many, the journey from addiction to recovery is marked by resilience and an unwavering commitment to reclaiming their lives. During these moments of vulnerability, the human spirit reveals its strength, demonstrating that transformation is possible even in the face of profound despair.**

Somewhere in the city, a survivor of domestic violence takes tentative steps toward a new path, uncertain yet determined. The journey is fraught with challenges, each day a testament to courage and determination. Breaking free from the grip of control and fear demands a strength that words can scarcely capture. It's about finding the courage to say, "No more," and the strength to rebuild from the ground up. These survivors, often with nothing but the clothes on their backs, embark on a quest of renewal, creating new lives rooted in freedom and empowerment. The process involves not only physical safety but also the healing of emotional scars. Support groups and therapy become lifelines, offering guidance and solidarity. These narratives of renewal highlight the resilience of the human spirit, where breaking free from the cycle of abuse becomes a powerful act of defiance and hope.

What is the catalyst for transformation? Often, the presence of a mentor or a moment of clarity ignites change. Mentors serve as beacons, offering guidance and a glimpse of a life beyond current struggles. **A mentor's belief in one's potential can be a motivation, instilling a sense of worth and possibility.** In other instances, a **personal revelation acts as a turning point**—an instance where clarity begins, and the path forward becomes clear. It might be a realization during a quiet moment of reflection or an event that shifts perspective. These turning points are unique to each individual, marking the beginning of a journey toward healing and growth. **They remind us that transformation is deeply personal, often arising from a blend of internal and external factors.**

The emotional and psychological aspects of transformation are profound, blending self-discovery and healing. Developing **self-compassion** is crucial in this process, allowing individuals to forgive themselves and embrace their fragility. It's about recognizing that mistakes do not define one's worth and that healing is a gradual, often complex process. **Forgiveness, both of oneself and others is equally important. It releases the hold of past grievances, freeing individuals to move forward without the heavy load they carry.** Transformation also involves rebuilding self-esteem, often eroded by years of addiction or abuse. It's about finding joy in small victories and celebrating progress, no matter how little it may seem. **As individuals navigate these emotional landscapes, they cultivate resilience and strength, emerging with a renewed sense of self.**

Take a moment to reflect on your own capacity for transformation. Consider where you feel stuck or helpless, and envision a path toward change. What could be the turning point that sets your journey in motion? It could be a mentor, a moment of clarity, or the decision to seek support. Embrace the possibility of transformation, knowing that change is within reach. Reflect on the emotional and psychological shifts required to move forward, and approach this journey with patience and self-compassion. **Transformation is not a destination; it's a process of continuous growth and renewal.** As you navigate your path, allow these stories of recovery and empowerment to inspire and guide you, illuminating the way forward.

7.5 LESSONS IN RESILIENCE FROM DIVERSE PERSPECTIVES

Resilience manifests differently across cultures, each providing unique insights into how communities endure hardship. Among Indigenous peoples, resilience is often deeply intertwined with belonging and connection to the land. Traditional practices and the wisdom of elders play a crucial role, providing a framework for strength and continuity. **These communities often rely on oral traditions and storytelling to pass down history and instill values that fortify their members against adversity.** Community cohesion is paramount, with collective support systems that bolster individuals, ensuring that no one stands alone in times of struggle. This cultural approach to resilience emphasizes the importance of interdependence, where one member's well-being is linked to all's well-being.

Across the globe, many cultures have built resilience through strong community-based support systems. In many African and Asian societies, communal living, often called "ubuntu" in some African cultures, highlights the belief in a universal bond that connects all humanity. This philosophy fosters resilience by encouraging individuals to lean on each other and share resources and responsibilities. Such support systems create a safety net that catches individuals when they fall, offering a sense of security that empowers them to take risks and face challenges without fear. These practices remind us that resilience is not solely an individual endeavor but a shared commitment to uplift and support one another.

The narratives of resilience from underrepresented voices also provide valuable lessons. Women in male-dominated industries often encounter systemic barriers, yet their resilience enables them to shatter glass ceilings. Their stories are tales of tenacity, where persistence and ingenuity pave the way for success. These women often rely on networks of mentorship and advocacy, forming alliances that amplify their voices and create pathways for future generations. Similarly, LGBTQ+ individuals, many of whom face societal discrimination, exhibit remarkable resilience. Their courage to live authentically, often in the face of adversity, showcases the power of self-acceptance and community support. **Their experiences highlight the importance of creating inclusive spaces where diversity is celebrated, and everyone is empowered to thrive.**

Resilience is not confined to any single stage of life; it evolves as we do. Young adults, for instance, navigate early career challenges with a resilience often fueled by ambition and adaptability. They face a rapidly changing job market, where uncertainty is the norm, yet they persist, seeking opportunities for growth and learning. For seniors, resilience might take the form of embracing new passions and redefining purpose post-retirement. Their stories reveal a resilience rooted in wisdom and experience, where life's transitions are seen as opportunities for reinvention rather than endings. These narratives remind us that resilience is a lifelong trait, adapting to the demands of each stage of life while drawing from the depths of our experiences.

To integrate these diverse lessons into personal growth, Embracing resilience means recognizing its communal nature—leaning on and uplifting those around you. Strengthen your resilience by immersing yourself in community—volunteer, participate in local events, and foster meaningful connections. Learn from the experiences of those around you, especially those whose voices are often marginalized. Their stories can provide new perspectives and inspire resilience in your own life. Additionally, reflect on how resilience manifests differently at various life stages and consider how you can apply these insights to your current circumstances. **By embracing a diverse understanding of resilience, you can cultivate a more holistic and adaptable approach to facing life's challenges.**

7.6 APPLYING INSIGHTS FROM INSPIRATIONAL STORIES

Imagine standing at a crossroads, faced with a decision that could transform your life. Though uncertainty looms, within you lies the power to conquer this fear through decisive action. The uncertainty is overwhelming, yet within you lies the potential to overcome this fear with decisive action. The essence of these stories is the courage to move forward, even when doubts linger. These narratives teach us that fear is not an impassable barrier but a challenge to be met with courage and resilience. By taking action, even in the most minor steps, you begin to diminish fear's power over you. **This insight is a powerful reminder that progress often starts with a single, brave step.**

Equally significant is the community's role in overcoming unbearable odds. The stories highlight how individuals, when supported by a nurturing community, find strength that transcends their capabilities. This shared resilience becomes a formidable force, one that inspires and uplifts. Whether through family, friends, or a network of like-minded individuals, the power of community lies in its ability to provide support, encouragement, and perspective. **In these connections, you find the courage to push beyond your perceived limits, knowing that you are not alone in your struggle.**

With these insights, you can develop a personal resilience plan tailored to your unique circumstances. Start by crafting a resilience toolkit—a personalized collection of resources, strategies, and practices to fortify your ability to face challenges head-on. This kit might include **mindfulness practices**, **stress-management techniques,** and a list of supportive contacts. These tools serve as your anchors, stabilizing you in turbulent times. Additionally, **set resilience-building goals** that challenge you to grow. Set specific, attainable goals that serve as your roadmap to building resilience, guiding your progress step by step. By approaching resilience as a skill to be cultivated, you empower yourself to navigate life's uncertainties confidently and gracefully.

Incorporating these lessons into your daily life involves practical steps that reinforce resilience. Start each morning with affirmations drawn from the stories of resilience that inspire you. Let these words ground you in your strength and potential, setting an empowering tone for the day ahead. Practice gratitude by acknowledging small successes, no matter how minor. **This habit shifts your focus from what's lacking to what's abundant, fostering a mindset of positivity and growth. Though simple, these practices profoundly impact your outlook and resilience, reinforcing the belief that you can overcome whatever challenges come your way.**

Sharing personal stories is another powerful tool for growth. **Sharing your experiences contributes to a tapestry of collective resilience, offering insights and inspiration to all who listen.** This exchange of stories fosters a sense of community and mutual support, where shared experiences become lessons for all. Encourage others to share their stories, weaving a tapestry of resilience that connects and fortifies each of you. This communal storytelling empowers individuals and builds bridges of understanding and empathy, enriching the lives of all involved.

As we close this chapter, consider how these insights can transform your life. Reflect on the stories that resonated with you—their lessons are seeds of wisdom. Cultivate these insights into your daily practices and mindset, nurturing your growth and resilience. **The resilience journey is ongoing, shaped by the stories we tell and our actions. Embrace the power of resilience, knowing you have the tools and support to thrive in adversity.**

As we journey onward, we will uncover how these narratives of strength and community can spark change and fuel innovation, guiding us toward a future brimming with possibility.

Storms and Strength: A Tale of Resilience:

The sky was dark, the winds ran wild,
A storm approached, both fierce and riled.
Yet duty called, we took our place,
Fear in our hearts, yet steady in grace.
Through trembling hands and silent doubt,
We learned what strength was all about.

The leaders stand, their course unknown,
Through winds of change, they steer alone.
Yet vision guides their weary sight,
Through endless storms, they find the light.
With empathy, they lift the crew,
And forge a path both bold and true.

A leader falls, yet rises high,
Anwar's tale won't say goodbye.
Through prison walls and trials vast,
He held his truth, his faith stood fast.
With justice carved in battle's wake,
He proved what hearts can bear and break.

A boy was born with limbs so few,
Yet in his soul, the fire grew.
He rose beyond what others saw,
And taught the world to dream, not thaw.
For strength is built where doubts reside,
And hope can turn the fear to pride.

The Hershey name, once built, then lost,
Through shattered dreams and heavy cost.

Yet from the dust, they dared to rise,
With toil and trust, they claimed the prize.
For those who bend but do not break,
Can carve their fate with what they make.

From helpless hands to hopeful light,
Through pain, through loss, through endless night.
Yet in each tale, a lesson gleams,
That courage lives in broken dreams.
For we, like them, must rise and stand,
And shape our fate with heart in hand.

8

ACHIEVING LONG-TERM TRANSFORMATION

"Embarking on my global journey, I began with airsickness pills in my purse and high heels on my feet, walking the airports for a decade. This first real job transformed me from a teenager into a mature adult. It was a period of cultural awakening as I ventured from the bustling souks of Karachi to the historic paths by the Arc de Triomphe in Paris, collecting colorful memories I hold dear. Throughout these travels, I broadened my horizons and fortified my emotional resilience, learning to navigate the complexities of diverse personalities. The challenge of enduring a week-long layover in Europe's picturesque yet demanding landscapes tested my stamina to say no to dinner invites from people I knew I shouldn't go with, revealing my strength. Despite the challenges of my early flying career, mostly overcoming the airsickness and getting used to mingling with people from all walks of life, it proved to be a pivotal stepping stone, enabling me to provide for my family and explore the globe—an opportunity that might have eluded me otherwise. This journey commenced with a leap of faith, applying for a job I hardly believed I would get. It marked my initiation into a world where joy and sorrow interlace, setting the stage for the profound transformations that awaited me."

8.1 SUSTAINING CHANGE THROUGH CONSISTENCY

Imagine a sculptor at work, chipping away at a block of marble, each chisel strike deliberate and measured. The transformation from stone to statue doesn't happen with a single blow. Instead, it results from consistent effort, where every small action contributes to the final masterpiece. In personal development, this sculpting metaphor is a potent reminder that long-term transformation is rooted in our daily, steady, persistent actions.

Consistency forms the foundation for new habits and practices in our daily lives. Much like the sculptor's methodical approach, **adopting a routine allows us to embed transformative habits into our existence.** Consistent actions, no matter how small, gradually accumulate, leading to significant growth and transformation over time. This approach builds momentum, making larger tasks feel more manageable and achievable. As we consistently train ourselves, we create a rhythm that sustains our efforts even during challenging times. **This rhythm becomes the backbone of habit formation, anchoring us as we navigate the complexities of change.**

The benefits of consistent effort extend beyond immediate results. Over time, consistency helps us maintain focus and reinforces our commitment to personal growth. By regularly engaging in exercise, reading, or mindfulness practices, we create a framework that supports development. This consistency allows us to track progress effectively, making adjusting our strategies easier. **Whether learning a new skill or pursuing a long-term goal, the steady application of effort ensures that we remain aligned with our aspirations.**

Building consistency in personal development requires practical strategies that integrate seamlessly into daily life. Establishing daily routines is a fundamental step in this process. By creating a structured schedule, we set aside dedicated time for activities that align with our goals. This structure eliminates the guesswork, providing a sense of predictability that fosters consistency. Using habit trackers can further enhance our efforts by visually representing our progress. These tools are tangible reminders of our commitment, motivating us to maintain our routines and celebrate our achievements.

Despite the best intentions, barriers to consistency often arise, threatening to derail our progress. Procrastination is a common obstacle that can hinder our ability to stay on track. It is essential to break tasks into manageable steps to combat this, focusing on one action at a time. Setting realistic expectations and celebrating small victories reduce the pressure that fuels procrastination. External distractions also pose a challenge to consistency. Managing these distractions involves creating an environment conducive to focus. This plan might mean setting boundaries with technology, designating quiet spaces for work, or scheduling specific times for focused activities. By minimizing interruptions, we protect the integrity of our routines, allowing us to maintain momentum.

Real-life examples illustrate the transformative power of consistency. Consider the story of an aspiring writer who committed to writing 500 words daily. Initially, progress seemed slow, but these daily efforts culminated in a completed manuscript over time. The act of writing became a habit ingrained in the routine of daily life. This consistency produced tangible results and reinforced the writer's identity as an author—similarly, a young professional seeking career advancement dedicated time each week to learning new skills online. She acquired valuable knowledge that propelled her career forward by consistently engaging in these educational pursuits. **These examples underscore that transformation is not a sudden event but the result of sustained deliberate action.**

<u>Interactive Element: Consistency Check-In</u>

To assist you in building consistency, consider implementing a weekly check-in to evaluate your progress. Dedicate weekly minutes to review your goals and reflect on your efforts. Use a journal or planner to note any challenges encountered and the strategies to overcome them. This practice encourages accountability and provides an opportunity to celebrate your successes. By regularly assessing your consistency, you gain insight into your habits and identify areas for improvement, ensuring that your efforts remain aligned with your long-term vision.

Consistency is the guiding force that propels us forward in pursuing long-term transformation. The steady application of effort shapes our habits and molds our character. As we embrace consistency in our personal development journey, we lay the groundwork for enduring change, creating a life that reflects our values and aspirations.

8.2 LONG-TERM STRATEGIES FOR EMOTIONAL GROWTH

Emotional growth is an ongoing, evolving process that enriches our lives by deepening our understanding of ourselves and our interactions with the world. While emotional intelligence is about recognizing and managing feelings, emotional maturity comes from experience—it's the ability to respond thoughtfully instead of reacting impulsively. The gradual development of this maturity forms the cornerstone of long-term transformation, guiding us through life's ups and downs with grace and resilience.

To cultivate this growth, **developing emotional self-awareness is vital.** This process involves consistently tuning into your feelings and understanding their origins. Regular emotional check-ins serve as a practical tool for this purpose. Setting aside time daily to reflect on your emotions makes you more attuned to your inner state. Ask yourself questions like, "What am I feeling right now?" and "What triggered this emotion?" These reflections illuminate patterns and insights, helping you respond more effectively to similar situations in the future. **Reflective journaling** complements this practice, providing a dedicated space to explore your emotional landscape. **By writing about your experiences and emotions, you gain clarity and perspective, uncovering more profound layers of understanding that might otherwise remain hidden.**

Building emotional agility is another crucial aspect of this process. This skill allows you to adapt your emotional responses to life's ever-changing circumstances. **It involves recognizing that emotions are not static but fluid, capable of evolving with your experiences.** Techniques for flexible emotional responses include pausing before reacting, considering alternative perspectives, and practicing empathy. These strategies enable you to navigate complex emotional situations with composure and understanding. For instance, when faced with criticism at work, instead of reacting defensively, take a moment to breathe and consider the feedback an opportunity for growth. **This approach fosters resilience, helping you maintain balance even in challenging scenarios.**

Emotional growth significantly impacts our relationships, enhancing the quality and depth of our connections. As you develop greater emotional self-awareness, you become more attuned to the emotions of those around you. The heightened sensitivity allows for more empathetic and compassionate interactions, fostering trust and understanding. Emotional maturity empowers you to communicate more effectively, clearly, and respectfully, expressing your needs and boundaries. It also equips you to handle conflicts constructively, seeking resolution rather than escalation. By nurturing emotional growth within your relationships, you create an environment where you and your loved ones can thrive.

Consider the transformative power of emotional growth in a relationship. Imagine a couple facing a disagreement about their plans. In the heat of the moment, emotions may run high, leading to misunderstandings and hurt feelings. However, with emotional maturity, both partners can navigate this conflict with empathy and openness. By actively listening to each other's perspectives and acknowledging their emotions, they create a safe space for honest dialogue. This process resolves the immediate issue and strengthens their bond, reinforcing trust and intimacy. **Relationships become resilient and supportive through emotional growth, capable of weathering life's inevitable challenges.**

Emotional growth is a guiding force in pursuing long-term transformation, shaping our responses, relationships, and overall well-being. We embark on a lifelong personal development journey by fostering emotional self-awareness, building agility, and nurturing connections. **This path enriches our individual lives and enhances the collective experience of those we share it with.**

8.3 CULTIVATING A LIFE OF PURPOSE AND MEANING

Imagine waking up each day with anticipation, knowing that your actions contribute to a cause, passion, or purpose greater than yourself. This feeling is often rooted in a life filled with purpose and meaning. To bring this sense of purpose into your own life, begin by **identifying what truly matters to you.** Reflect on moments when you felt alive and fulfilled. Was it while expressing yourself through a creative project, making a difference in someone's life, or discovering new ideas that sparked your curiosity? Such experiences provide valuable insights into your passions and core values. Engage in exercises that help uncover these passions—like analyzing what interests you or creating a list that captures your dreams and aspirations. Such practices can illuminate the path toward what fuels your spirit and brings you joy.

Once you've identified your sources of purpose, the next step is to **integrate them into your daily life.** This change is not about making grand gestures but aligning your routine with your values. Consider how your daily tasks can reflect your long-term goals. For example, if you find meaning in helping others, look for opportunities to volunteer or support a cause you care about. If creativity is your driving force, carve out time daily to engage in artistic pursuits, whether writing, painting, or playing music. These small, deliberate actions can transform mundane routines into meaningful endeavors, grounding your life in purpose.

Setting purpose-driven goals is another powerful way to infuse your life with meaning. Start by crafting a personal mission statement encapsulating your core values and aspirations. This statement is a guiding star, helping you navigate decisions and stay true to what matters most. From there, set specific milestones that align with your mission. These can be short-term goals that offer immediate satisfaction or long-term objectives that require sustained effort. For example, if your purpose involves fostering community, a short-term goal might be organizing a local event, while a long-term milestone could be developing a community-based project. Setting and pursuing these goals creates a blueprint for a life that reflects your deepest intentions.

Consider the stories of individuals who have embraced purpose-driven lives. Take, for instance, a teacher who found profound fulfillment in nurturing young minds. Her purpose extended beyond imparting knowledge; she aimed to inspire curiosity and a love for learning in her students. This sense of purpose guided her teaching philosophy, influencing her approach to education and creating a lasting impact on her students. Or think of an entrepreneur who built a business centered on sustainability. The goal is to commit to environmental stewardship that weaves into every aspect of his company, from product design to corporate culture. By aligning his work with his values, he achieved professional success and contributed to a cause he sincerely believed in.

These examples illustrate that purpose-driven lives are not confined to specific roles or careers. They are accessible to anyone willing to explore their passions and align their actions accordingly. Whether you're a caregiver, artist, scientist, or entrepreneur, the potential for purpose exists within every facet of life. **It begins with a willingness to reflect on what truly matters and the courage to pursue it with intention.** Doing so creates a fulfilling and prosperous life with meaning and impact.

8.4 EMBRACING VULNERABILITY AS STRENGTH

Imagine facing a moment of exposure—your heart pounding, palms sweaty, and a thousand thoughts racing through your mind. In that moment, vulnerability is palpable. It's the raw, unfiltered exposure of your innermost self to the world. Traditionally, society has conditioned us to see vulnerability as a weakness—something to be concealed rather than embraced. Yet, in truth, vulnerability is a profound source of strength. It serves as a catalyst for genuine connection, igniting authenticity in relationships, workplaces, and personal growth. When we allow ourselves to be vulnerable, we open the door to deeper, more meaningful interactions. **In being vulnerable, we invite others to see us as we are, fostering an environment where trust and empathy can flourish.**

To embrace vulnerability, we must first challenge the long-held belief that it equates to fragility. Vulnerability is not about indiscriminately exposing every part of ourselves but about **choosing to be open in safe and nurturing spaces**. One practice that encourages this openness is sharing personal stories in environments with abundant understanding and support. Whether confiding in a trusted friend or expressing ourselves in a supportive group, these sharing moments allow us to explore our vulnerabilities without fear of judgment. **They remind us that our stories, with all their imperfections, hold value and power.**

Engaging in honest self-reflection is another practice that nurtures vulnerability. This focus involves looking inward, acknowledging our fears, insecurities, and desires without the need for pretense. Self-reflection is not about criticizing ourselves but understanding the layers that make us human. **In these quiet moments of introspection, we often find the courage to face our vulnerabilities openly.** By embracing this process, we cultivate a deeper awareness of who we are, empowering us to engage with the world more authentically.

In relationships, vulnerability serves as the foundation for deeper connections and trust. It binds us to one another, creating bonds of authenticity and mutual respect. We invite others to do the same when we communicate openly and honestly. Techniques for open-hearted communication, such as active listening and expressing our needs clearly, pave the way for this exchange. They create a space where both parties feel heard and validated, even when disagreements arise. **By prioritizing vulnerability in our interactions, we build resilient and enduring relationships capable of withstanding the tests of time.**

Consider the story of a woman who, after years of hiding her true feelings, chose to share her struggles with her partner. Initially, the fear of rejection seemed significant, but as she voiced her experiences, she found a sense of relief. Her vulnerability became a bridge, allowing her partner to understand her fully. In turn, this openness inspired him to share his own challenges, strengthening their connection. They discovered a newfound strength in their relationship through vulnerability, built on trust and shared understanding.

Similarly, a young professional who once feared public speaking found empowerment through vulnerability. By admitting her anxiety to her colleagues and seeking their support, she transformed her perceived weakness into a source of strength. With encouragement and practice, she embraced opportunities to speak, gradually building confidence and resilience. Her vulnerability empowered her and inspired others to confront their fears.

These stories illustrate that vulnerability is not a hindrance but a powerful force for personal growth and connection. When we allow ourselves to be vulnerable, we embrace the fullness of our humanity. We acknowledge that imperfection is not something to hide but a testament to our uniqueness. **In this acceptance, we find strength, resilience, and the courage to live authentically. Vulnerability invites us to connect deeply with others, share our stories and experiences, and build lives enriched by understanding and empathy.**

8.5 THE JOURNEY TO AUTHENTIC EMPOWERMENT

Authentic empowerment is a profound concept, contrasting sharply with superficial empowerment, which often masquerades as genuine strength through external validation and temporary achievements. While superficial empowerment may rely on external validation and fleeting successes, **authentic empowerment is deeply rooted in self-awareness and**

purpose. It emerges from understanding one's values, strengths, and passions and thrives in alignment with one's true self. When authentically empowered, you draw unwavering strength from within, guided by an inner compass that remains steadfast amid life's challenges.

The path to authentic empowerment begins with building **self-trust** and **self-reliance**—two foundational elements that enable you to move forward confidently in your journey. **Trusting yourself** means having confidence in your ability to navigate challenges, whether it's making tough decisions at work or standing firm in your values during difficult situations. It involves acknowledging your strengths and weaknesses and using them as guides rather than constraints. **Self-reliance** grows from this trust, allowing you to take initiative and assume responsibility for your actions. **As you cultivate these qualities, your confidence grows, enabling you to shape your life according to your desires—free from needing constant approval from others.**

Embracing your narrative is another essential step, as it allows you to reclaim your story and use it as a tool for empowerment. **Your story's unique experiences and lessons are a testament to your resilience and growth.** Accepting and celebrating your journey empowers you to move forward with authenticity, living a life true to who you are. This realization involves letting go of the narratives imposed by others and crafting your own. It means recognizing that every chapter, even the challenging ones, contributes to the person you are becoming. **In this acceptance, you find empowerment, allowing you to write your narrative with clarity, intention, and purpose.**

Self-expression plays a pivotal role in authentic empowerment. By communicating your values and aspirations, you can open opportunities that align with your authentic self. Creative outlets like writing, painting, or music offer unique paths for self-discovery, unlocking different facets of your inner self. They allow you to explore and articulate what matters most, fostering a deeper connection with your inner self. Public speaking, too, serves as a platform for sharing your truths and inspiring others. By voicing your experiences and insights, you empower yourself and create ripples of change that can inspire those around you.

Sustaining authentic empowerment over time requires continual learning and adaptation. The world is ever-changing, and so are we. By committing to lifelong learning, you remain open to new ideas and perspectives, allowing your empowerment to evolve alongside you. This adaptability ensures that your empowerment is resilient and can withstand the tests of time and circumstance. Seeking empowering environments and communities further supports this journey. Surrounding yourself with individuals who uplift and inspire you creates a network of support that nurtures your empowerment. These connections provide encouragement and accountability, helping you stay true to your path.

As you navigate this journey, remember that **empowerment is not a destination but a state of being.** It is a dynamic, ever-evolving process that requires patience and perseverance. This empowerment becomes a guiding light, illuminating your path and enabling you to navigate life's complexities with confidence and grace.

> The essence of authentic empowerment lies in its ability to transform not only your life but also the lives of those around you. As you embody your true self, you inspire others to do the same, creating a ripple effect that extends far beyond your individual experience.
>
> This way, authentic empowerment catalyzes positive change within and beyond, setting the stage for continued exploration and growth.

KEEPING THE STRENGTH ALIVE

Now that you have everything you need to **build resilience, overcome self-doubt, and ignite your inner strength**, it's time to share your journey and help others find the same courage.

Simply by leaving your opinion of this book on Amazon, you'll show other **people who feel lost, uncertain, or in need of hope** where they can find the guidance they're looking for—and inspire them to take action.

Your review isn't just feedback—it's a beacon of encouragement for someone searching for their own inner strength.

Thank you for your help. **Resilience grows stronger when we pass on what we've learned**—and you're helping to keep that spirit alive.

With my sincerest gratitude,
Arlene Grace Evangelista

CONCLUSION

As we conclude this journey, let's revisit the core themes that have guided us through this book: courage, overcoming self-doubt, resilience, and emotional intelligence, all of which intertwine to create lasting empowerment. Each chapter illuminates these pillars, offering pathways to transform personal challenges into opportunities for growth. **This book aims to shift the narrative from feelings of helplessness and isolation to one of empowerment, guiding you to focus on what truly matters.**

Reflecting on our path together, I encourage you to pause and reflect on the profound transformation you've experienced. We started by exploring emotional intelligence and how it can shape your emotional responses and relationships. From there, we delved into fostering a growth mindset; we examined how embracing life's challenges head-on can strengthen your resilience and empower you to face future obstacles. You've made profound progress toward personal empowerment, conquering self-doubt, and mastering the art of navigating transitions.

The strategies and lessons in these pages are not just theories; they are actionable tools designed to create real change in your life. We discussed building emotional intelligence through daily practices, adopting a growth mindset to face challenges head-on, and overcoming self-doubt with cognitive techniques. Navigating life's transitions became more empowering and intentional with the help of structured decision-making frameworks and supportive community building. You learned to find balance and serenity amidst chaos through mindfulness, while real-life narratives offered inspiration and practical insights.

Throughout this book, you've been equipped with practical exercises, actionable techniques, and powerful frameworks designed to be used every day. From emotional check-ins to mindfulness meditation, these strategies have been your allies in fostering emotional courage. Let these insights become your daily habits, propelling you toward lasting personal growth and empowerment.

Your commitment to this journey deserves recognition. By engaging with this book, you've taken commendable steps toward emotional courage and resilience. It's a process, and your progress is both ongoing and admirable. Celebrate your achievements, however small they seem, and acknowledge your cultivated strength.

This book can be your companion for continuous learning and inspiration. Revisit sections that resonate with you, and share your experiences with others who may benefit from these insights. Building a supportive network is crucial, so engage with communities that foster growth and mutual support. These connections will fortify your resilience and enrich your journey.

As you continue this path, I urge you to take immediate action. Set specific goals aligned with your values and approach them with **courage and resilience. Your journey is not just about reading; it's about doing and taking tangible steps that reflect the insights gained. Let this be a call to action that propels you into a life of purpose and strength.**

I am deeply thankful for your engagement and commitment to this book. Each concept you've embraced, and every page you've turned have significantly contributed to our shared journey, making it incredibly meaningful to me. My heartfelt gratitude goes out to you for allowing me to be a part of your path toward discovery and growth. I sincerely hope that the insights within these pages serve you well across the varied landscapes of your life. Remember, within you lies the formidable power to navigate obstacles and prioritize what is truly significant. The road to emotional courage is replete with opportunities, and I am confident in your ability to foster enduring resilience.

Let the key takeaway be this: **You are empowered, motivated, and prepared to face life's challenges with courage and resilience. Embrace this newfound strength, trusting your capacity to grow and thrive in all areas of life.**

"Years have elapsed since I held those little hands...

You and I probably hold or want to hold someone's hands, whether a loved one, a family member, a friend, or even a stranger. We may not fully understand the depths of their sorrow or the weight of their pain, but we want to be there for them. But first, we need to have courage within us before we touch someone else's hands. How can we share hope if we feel lost? How can we give something that we don't have? How can we convince someone to be strong if we are not?

Let us muster our emotional courage for ourselves and for others. Let's embrace our fears and vulnerabilities so we can help others carry theirs.

We can find courage.

We are stronger than we realize. Giving up is not our path.

Let's open our hearts, touch lives, and hold on to what truly matters.

With so much love,

Always."

A JOURNEY'S END, A NEW BEGINNING

The road we've walked was paved with fire,
With doubt and fear, with hope, desire.
Yet through it all, we dared to stand,
To shape our fate with steady hands.
From storms of loss to skies so bright,
We found our strength, we claimed our light.

Emotions taught us how to bend,
To break, rebuild, to rise again.
With hearts aware and minds refined,
We learned to see, to heal, to find.
For growth is not in ease or rest,
But in the trials we've faced, confessed.

Through self-doubt's whispers, loud and cruel,
We forged our path, reclaimed the rules.
Resilience wrapped us, bold and true,
A guiding force in all we do.
No step was lost, no pain in vain,
Each wound became the source of gain.

The lessons here, not words alone,
But tools to carve a life our own.
To meet our fears with steady grace,
To move with purpose, claim our space.
For courage lives where love resides,
A flame that burns, a force that guides.

And now we stand with hands stretched wide,
Not just for us—but those denied.
For how can hope be freely shared,
If first within, it's not declared?
So let us love, let fear depart,
With open hands and fearless heart.

This is not where the story ends,
But where the path of courage bends.
With every choice, with every fight,
We shape our future, claim our might.
So walk ahead—unchained, untamed,
Your life, your fire, forever claimed.

REFERENCES

Emotional Intelligence and Resilience

Greater Good Science Center. (n.d.). *Evidence mounts that mindfulness breeds resilience*. University of California, Berkeley. https://greatergood.berkeley.edu/article/item/evidence_mounts_that_mindfulness_breeds_resilience

HuffPost. (2013, December 20). *5 resilience traits we can all learn from Nelson Mandela*. https://www.huffpost.com/entry/nelson-mandela-legacy_b_4466636

Marler, T. (2024, April 8). *Overcoming adversity: Inspiring stories of resilience and growth*. LinkedIn. https://www.linkedin.com/pulse/overcoming-adversity-inspiring-stories-resilience-tania-marler-mba-nyjce

National Center for Biotechnology Information. (n.d.). *A new layered model on emotional intelligence*. National Institutes of Health. https://pmc.ncbi.nlm.nih.gov/articles/PMC5981239/

Talend. (n.d.). *Finding certainty in uncertain times: 3 success stories*. https://www.talend.com/blog/finding-certainty-in-uncertain-times-3-success-stories/

Ungar, M. (2006, October 18). *Resilience across cultures*. The British Journal of Social Work, *38*(2), 218–235. https://academic.oup.com/bjsw/article/38/2/218/1684596

Vocal Media. (2023). *Triumph over adversity: 10 inspiring stories of resilience and success*. https://vocal.media/humans/triumph-over-adversity-10-inspiring-stories-of-resilience-and-success

NPR. (2022, November 24). *From prisoner to prime minister, Malaysia's Anwar had long ride to top*. NPR. https://www.npr.org/2022/11/24/1139144583/reformist-leader-anwar-named-prime-minister-of-malaysia

Wikipedia contributors. (n.d.). *Nick Vujicic*. In *Wikipedia, The Free Encyclopedia*. Retrieved January 28, 2025, from https://en.wikipedia.org/wiki/Nick_Vujicic

The Top Business Schools and Degrees. (n.d.). *10 Millionaire Entrepreneurs Who Bounced Back From Bankruptcy*. The Top Business Schools and Degrees.

Pasela by Positive Action. (n.d.). *Word of the Week: Courage*. Pasela by Positive Action. https://www.pasela.com/word-of-the-week/courage

Mindfulness and Self-Reflection

TalktoAngel. (2024, September 10). *8 ways to practice self-reflection: A path to personal growth*. https://www.talktoangel.com/blog/8-ways-to-practice-self-reflection-a-path-to-personal-growth

Mindfulness Exercises. (2020, December 12). *How mindfulness builds resilience: What science says*. https://mindfulnessexercises.com/how-mindfulness-builds-resilience-what-science-says/

Nemko, M. (2019, July 13). *Journaling for personal growth*. Psychology Today. https://www.psychologytoday.com/us/blog/how-to-do-life/201907/journaling-for-personal-growth

Mayo Clinic News Network. (2019, May 29). *Mayo mindfulness: Overcoming negative self-talk*. Mayo Clinic. https://newsnetwork.mayoclinic.org/discussion/mayo-mindfulness-overcoming-negative-self-talk/

National Center for Biotechnology Information. (2020). *The effectiveness of mindfulness-based stress reduction*. National Institutes of Health. https://pmc.ncbi.nlm.nih.gov/articles/PMC7511255/

Keep Inspiration Alive. (2024). *Mindful living: Simple practices to reduce stress and increase happiness*. Retrieved from https://www.keepinspirationalive.com/post/mindful-living-simple-practices-to-reduce-stress-and-increase-happiness

Studio 42 Co. (2024, July 19). *Learn how meditation can improve your mental health*. Retrieved from https://studio42co.com/blog/learn-how-meditation-can-improve-your-mental-health

Sierra Summit 2005. (n.d.). *Embracing the natural beauty: A journey into the wonders of nature*. Retrieved from https://sierrasummit2005.org/uncategorized/natural/

Star Glowe. (2024). *Embracing Global Wellness Day: A path to a healthier, happier life*. Retrieved from https://starglowe.com/embracing-global-wellness-day-a-path-to-a-healthier-happier-life/

Top News Insiders. (2024). The art of mindfulness: Finding peace in a hectic world. Retrieved from https://topnewsinsiders.com/the-art-of-mindfulness-finding-peace-in-a-hectic-world/

Personal Growth and Goal Setting

Positive Psychology. (2020). *How to develop empathy: 10 exercises & worksheets*. https://positivepsychology.com/empathy-worksheets/

Mindset Works. (n.d.). *Decades of scientific research that started a growth mindset revolution*. https://www.mindsetworks.com/science/

King, J. (n.d.). *How to set purpose-driven goals*. https://www.janelleaking.com/blog/purpose-driven-goal-setting

MindTools. (n.d.). *How to write SMART goals, with examples*. https://www.mindtools.com/a4wo118/smart-goals

Kutsko Consulting. (n.d.). *Mastering self-awareness: Strategies for personal insight*. https://www.kutskoconsulting.com/blog/self-awareness-strategies

Nawaz, M. (2024, November 25). *The power of consistency in personal development. Medium.* https://medium.com/@muhammadnawaz.mn980/the-power-of-consistency-in-personal-development-05589f4c9878

The Dad Train. (2021, April 13). *How to develop a growth mindset, with Matthew Turner* (No. 48) [Audio podcast episode]. In *The Dad Train.* https://podcasts.apple.com/us/podcast/how-to-develop-a-growth-mindset-with-matthew-turner/id1508257421?i=1000517004294

Eng, B. (n.d.). *Having mindset growth to unleash your superpower. Bernard Eng.* https://bernardeng.com/blogs/having-mindset-growth-to-unleash-your-superpower/

Liezl. (2023). *Incorporating a growth mindset to live a fulfilling life. Liezl Asis.* https://www.liezlasis.com/post/growth-mindset-living-fulfilling-life

Saunders, J. (2023, July 19). *Why is growth mindset important. Jamie Saunders Coaching.* https://www.jamiesaunderscoaching.com/why-is-growth-mindset-important/

Byers, G. (2023, July 12). *When failing beats perfection. Geoffrey Byers.* https://geoffreybyers.com/when-failing-beats-perfection/

Madison Niche Marketing. (2021, April 27). *How to cultivate a growth mindset and thrive as a software engineer. Madison Niche Marketing.* https://madison-niche-marketing.com/2023/01/19/how-to-cultivate-a-growth-mindset-and-thrive-as-a-software-engineer

Sandjest. (2024). *120+ quotes about learning that will motivate you. Personalized Gift Sandjest.* https://sandjest.com/blogs/quotes/quotes-about-learning

Moore, W. (2023, December 15). *What is habitual thinking? A science-based guide to hit the reset button on your brain.* Moore Momentum. https://mooremomentum.com/blog/what-is-habitual-thinking/

Hormozi, A. (2024, March 24). The hack for patience. *Hormozi Blog.* https://hormozi.blog/the-hack-for-patience/

Neuroscience and Behavioral Change

Santa Fe Institute. (2023). *Conceptual framework for how societies adapt to change.* https://www.santafe.edu/news-center/news/new-conceptual-framework-may-help-scientists-understand-how-societies-adapt-change

UNESCO International Bureau of Education. (2019). *Neuroplasticity: How the brain changes with learning.* https://solportal.ibe-unesco.org/articles/neuroplasticity-how-the-brain-changes-with-learning/

Bridge Care ABA. (2024). *Positive reinforcement in ABA therapy.* Bridge Care ABA. Retrieved January 28, 2025, from https://www.bridgecareaba.com/blog/positive-reinforcement-in-aba-therapy

Shoorah. (n.d.). *The power of promises to yourself: How consistent daily rituals support confidence and well-being.* Shoorah. Retrieved January 28, 2025, from https://shoorah.io/the-power-of-promises-to-yourself-how-consistent-daily-rituals-support-confidence-and-well-being/

SelfConcept.com. (2024). *How to make difficult decisions with confidence.* Retrieved from https://selfconcept.com/blog/b/How-to-make-difficult-decisions-with-confidence

Relationships and Social Connectivity

Johnson, S. (2020, May 14). *How CEOs can lead selflessly through a crisis. Harvard Business Review.* https://hbr.org/2020/05/how-ceos-can-lead-selflessly-through-a-crisis

BetterHelp. (2024). *How to build a community: Strategies for fostering inclusion and support.* https://www.betterhelp.com/advice/how-to/how-to-build-a-community-strategies-for-fostering-inclusion-and-support

Hurlemann, R., & Scheele, D. (2018). *Oxytocin and social relationships: From attachment to bond maintenance. National Institutes of Health.* https://pmc.ncbi.nlm.nih.gov/articles/PMC5815947/

Haslam, C., Jetten, J., Cruwys, T., Dingle, G. A., & Haslam, S. A. (2022). *Social connectedness as a determinant of mental health. National Institutes of Health.* https://pmc.ncbi.nlm.nih.gov/articles/PMC9560615/

Rusnak, K. (2022, March 9). *The importance of vulnerability in healthy relationships*. Psychology Today. https://www.psychologytoday.com/us/blog/happy-healthy-relationships/202203/the-importance-of-vulnerability-in-healthy-relationships

Adamson, A. (n.d.). *DISCUSSION: Developing and Leveraging Brand Voice in Marketing (part 5 of 6)*. PPC Profit Pros. Retrieved from https://ppcprofitpros.com/discussion-developing-and-leveraging-brand-voice-in-marketing-part-5-of-6/

Practical Tools and Strategies

Indeed Editorial Team. (2024). *5 conflict resolution strategies: Steps, benefits, and tips*. Indeed. https://www.indeed.com/career-advice/career-development/conflict-resolution-strategies

BetterUp. (2021). *5 visualization techniques to help you reach your goals*. https://www.betterup.com/blog/visualization

New Hope Mental Health Counseling Services. (n.d.). *Harnessing the power of visualization: How imagery can improve mental well-being*. https://www.thenewhopemhcs.com/harnessing-the-power-of-visualization/

My Therapist Online. (n.d.). *Overcome self-doubt with proven CBT and ACT strategies*. https://www.mytherapistonline.co.uk/blog-notlinked/empowering-cbt-and-act-strategies-to-overcome-self-doubt-a-comprehensive-guide

HHRC. (2023). *Self-care assessment tool*. https://hhrctraining.org/knowledge-resources/article/3044/self-care-assessment-tool

Doctor Kevin. (2023, August 10). *The 5-step framework for decision-making in life transitions: Enhancing personal and professional growth*. Medium. https://doctorkevin.medium.com/the-5-step-framework-for-decision-making-in-life-transitions-enhancing-personal-and-professional-cacb659144b8

Henry Ford Health. (2017, May 24). *6 strategies for coping with change*. https://www.henryford.com/blog/2017/05/coping-with-change

www.ingramcontent.com/pod-product-compliance
Lightning Source LLC
Chambersburg PA
CBHW020426010526
44118CB00010B/441